BUILDING THE

CORPORATE

LEADERSHIP

COMMUNITY

Endorsements

This latest contribution to leadership by Anton and Letitia will not disappoint. Well-researched and authenticated by a number of thought-provoking case studies, it makes for a compelling read. Leaders, novice or experienced, will appreciate the fresh (and refreshed) insights and cohesive frameworks advocated by the authors – who are once again unafraid to look at the world differently and have the courage to do different things and write about them.

Michelle Ally, Programme Manager: The Academy@Work,
University of Johannesburg

The reflection on the new leadership landscape and the corporate leadership community is very valuable in that it provides a foundation from which to create leadership brand-enabling conditions and spot leadership talent. New leadership development approaches are suggested with the shift from leader development to leadership capacity-building. The book explores the important aspect of measurement of leadership and concludes with insightful case studies.

The one thing we know about the future of leadership development is that it is going to be different after this book, which manages to create a common purpose and shared meaning for organisational leadership.

Suretha Esterhuysen, Learning & Development: Momentum Short-term Insurance

Any corporation that believes in leadership development should embark on a journey to read this book. It is written by people who think differently and who challenge mind-sets. The authors will inspire their readers to change the way they do things and build the capability to ensure the leadership community is ready to take on the challenges of the future. The book is different to any other book on leadership you have read before; it stretches the mind and encourages thinking.

All industries are facing challenges and there is a lack of great leaders who inspire, motivate, develop, think differently and look for a 'team of rivals'. Look at the pearls of wisdom shared here and incorporate the thinking given in this book to ensure you have future leaders that will take leadership to a level never seen before.

Daleen Janse van Rensburg, Assistant Executive:
Operations: In-Touch Contact Centre (Outbound) Innovation Group

BUILDING THE CORPORATE

LEADERSHIP

COMMUNITY

*Creating a common purpose for and shared
meaning of organisational leadership*

Letitia van der Merwe
with Anton Verwey

kr
publishing

2016

First published in 2016

ISBN: 978-1-86922-581-0
eISBN: 978-1-86922-582-7 (PDF eBook)

Published by KR Publishing
P O Box 3954
Randburg
2125
Republic of South Africa

Tel: (011) 706-6009
Fax: (011) 706-1127
E-mail: orders@knowres.co.za
Website: www.kr.co.za

Printed and bound: Mega Digital (Pty) Ltd. Parow Industria, Cape Town
Typesetting, layout and design: Cia Joubert, cia@knowres.co.za
Cover design: Marlene de Villiers, marlene@knowres.co.za
Editing and proofreading: Jill Bishop, jill.bishop@absamail.co.za
Project management: Cia Joubert, cia@knowres.co.za

Table of Contents

Acknowledgements

Our heartfelt gratitude and appreciation go to the following people:

- Our colleagues at the inavit iQ group of companies for being true ambassadors of building a leadership community

- Our clients and partners, who through the years were not only true collaborators but also became friends. Thank you for sharing the insight into your organisations with our readers.

- To KR for making the dream of this book a reality

About the authors

Dr Letitia van der Merwe dedicates herself to exploring new ways to build better organisational talent capacity, especially leadership talent. Her career encompasses experiences from a wide range of leadership and organisational development projects and interventions in the private and public sector as well as in the world of consulting. She is an industrial psychologist by profession and combines the worlds of development and psychology. Letitia has published numerous articles and is the co-author of the book *Reshaping Leadership DNA*. Currently she is the managing director of inavit iQ learning. www.inavitiqlearning.com

Dr Anton Verwey takes a different perspective on the much-studied subject of leadership, focusing on leadership instead of on the individual leader. He has experience in a wide range of industries in the fields of Business Strategy, Organisation and Work Architecture, Leadership Talent Development and Human Capital processes and systems. For the past two decades his focus has been primarily on leadership capacity-building strategies. In this context, he has worked with organisations ranging from SMEs to listed companies, as well as some state-owned enterprises. He is the author and co-author of numerous books and articles and has supervised a number of master's and doctoral studies. Anton is the executive chairman of inavit iQ and also oversees the Business Development and Solutions Crafting portfolios for the group. www.inavitiq.com

About the contributors

Dr Charles du Toit has spent a significant part of his career in HR, mastering all aspects of the field and filling executive HR positions at a number of multi-national and local companies. In these roles he has become increasingly convinced that without connected leadership in organisations, the HR function is largely ineffective. He has a passion for leadership and strategic HR, presenting papers and consulting on a wide range of leadership and strategic HR projects. He works with individuals and companies developing their unique leadership brands. Charles is currently an executive consultant at Global Business Solutions, the HR Director of Eveready (Pty) Ltd and co-founder and chair of the Nelson Mandela Bay HR forum. He also lectures on leadership at the Nelson Mandela Metropolitan University Business School.

Ronel Minnaar has spent a significant part of her career working as a Leadership and Organisational Development manager within the mining industry. Her focus for the past decade has been primarily on leadership talent identification and leadership capacity-building strategies, which she continues to explore. She also works with leadership to build and maintain a culture and practice of high performance and resilience within the organisation to deal effectively with turbulent and challenging times. She is an industrial psychologist by profession and combines the worlds of leadership and psychology.

Yolandi Havemann focuses on the design of work and organisations (process and structure) to ensure people can be efficiently and effectively tasked, managed and developed to perform. She holds a BPsych (Hons) in Psychology and MCom in Industrial Psychology from the University of Pretoria, and has also completed certification in Business Process Redesign and Improvement. She has been in the consulting business for more than 10 years, working on business and organisation architecture projects in both the public and private sectors. Her work with client systems is strongly influenced by systems theory and the principles of requisite organisation.

About the contributor

Chapter 1

Oh no, not another book on leadership

Letitia van der Merwe and Anton Verwey

❄

"To expand leadership capacity, organisations must not only develop the leadership capacities of individuals but also develop the leadership capacity of collectives."
Ellen van Velsor & Cynthia McCauley

"Time is a structured perception towards observable changes." — **Toba Beta**

A while ago we had a conversation with one of our clients. They implemented a well-thought-through leadership development approach for their senior leaders. The programme included participation in social learning networks and reflective leadership journalling, and utilised an enquiry-based team process (an ongoing cycle of enquiry: question, investigate, reflect, and improve). Excellent results were obtained in terms of the feedback received from the senior leaders who participated in the programme. A year later our client realised that nothing had changed. Maybe it is a bit unfair to say that nothing had changed – individual leaders did grow and some behavioural changes were observed.

But in the end the realisation came that

1. some leaders knew what to say or do but were not willing to experience the discomfort, risk and uncertainty of saying or doing it and

2. this programme could just not create sufficient critical mass to support the leadership development intent.

> The legitimacy of management (and leadership) is under fire as never before. Fundamental questions are raised about why managers/leaders act and feel empowered to act in the ways they do. This is coupled with significant debate around the impact and effectiveness of leadership development. Some of the research indicates that there is dissatisfaction with the results of leadership development, while questions are also being asked about the way we develop leaders. In our own interaction with clients we hear similar arguments. It's as if organisations assume that if we show leaders what to do they will automatically do it. Our cognitive biases often lead us astray, particularly when we have to make big, difficult (and painful) choices.

Somehow it also seems that current leadership development programmes are not able to equip leaders with the necessary skills and tools to deal with the current volatile, ambiguous and complex business environment.

We think the challenge rests not only in leadership development. Leadership development should form part of an integrated view of leadership. We know that the days of the individual heroic leader who could inspire organisations are numbered. We know that the demanding complex business world requires leadership that is able to create shared possible futures with, through and for people. The future forms the context from which leadership derives justification for and meaning on why and how to act. Leadership is seen more and more as a social process that engages everyone in the community, but organisations have traditionally focused on developing individuals so that they can become better leaders – hence the concept "leader development". We even refer to individual development plans, putting the emphasis on individual learning. It clearly does not make sense to focus only on developing individual leaders, and there seems to be a growing recognition that the emphasis should be on developing leadership as a collective. What we envisage is that the future might very well be about developing leadership communities and networks of leaders.

Given these trends, we need to rethink how we define leadership beyond the "leader"; create a leadership brand that has "bankable" value; and create congruence between internal and external perceptions of leadership. Our own sense is that, in addition to the above, the future challenge is to create a community of leaders able and willing to lead organisations through the turbulence of an increasingly complex world.

So this is not a book that will necessarily make you a better leader. Nor does it contain the ultimate truth on leadership. As a matter of fact some of the things we are saying are not new; some of the ideas have been around for a while. The difference is that we want to focus not only on the concepts, but also on the practical application. Manfred Kets de Vries tells a wonderful story of a frog that was lying on a log in a river. Because the log was surrounded by alligators, the frog was at a loss to know how he could cross the river unharmed. At one point, he looked up at a tree and saw an owl sitting on a nearby branch. He said, "Wise owl, please help me. How can I cross this river without being eaten by the alligators?" The owl said, "That's very simple. Just flap your legs as much as you can. That should do it. That will make you fly, help you cross the river, and keep you out of reach of the alligators." The frog did as suggested, and just before he fell into the water, to be snapped up by one of the alligators, he asked the owl, "Why, *why* did you give me this advice? I'm going to be eaten." To which the owl responded, "My apologies. I'm only into concepts. Implementation of the concepts is not my cup of tea."

We also tend to view the world through our own lenses and make sense of it through very specific thinking frameworks. We think it is appropriate to share with you the sense-making frameworks that have informed and influenced our thinking on leadership through the years. We tend to combine two major disciplines:

- first, the systems theory sciences and more specifically the theories of Requisite Organisations and Levels of Work
- second, the world of psychology and more specifically the psychoanalytical paradigm

Why is leadership so important?

In our own experience many organisations find themselves experiencing significant leadership competency gaps, relying on an ever-narrowing base of managers who are sufficiently skilled to enact new managerial roles. We have also found that a wide range of social and business influences determines the leadership behaviour within an organisation. The challenges faced by leaders and organisations today are increasingly complex. The words "volatile", "multi-dimensional" and "unprecedented" are just a few that leaders use when discussing these challenges.

Research and our own experience have demonstrated that organisations with the highest-quality leaders are simply more likely to outperform their competition in key bottom-line metrics such as financial performance, quality of products and services, employee engagement and customer satisfaction. Figure 1.1 demonstrates this concept.

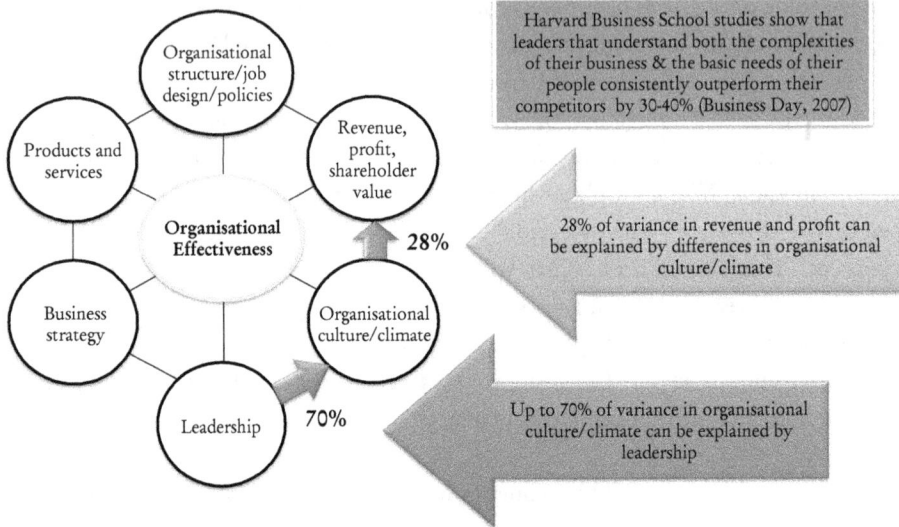

Figure 1.1 Impact of high-quality leadership[1]
(Adapted from Hay McBer's model of Organisational effectiveness)

Introducing key issues

In this book we focus on:

1. the difference between leaders and leadership. We introduce the concept of building a corporate leadership community and demonstrate that it is critical that the make-up, dynamics and evolution of leadership communities are clearly understood and managed. Associated with the leadership community is a certain leadership culture and climate: the interpersonal, team and organisation-wide dynamics amongst the organisation's leadership.

2. understanding that leaders are people too. Traditionally leadership development focuses on closing the competence/behavioural gaps identified by some sort of assessment. We argue that we first need to focus on understanding that leaders are not always these beacons of rationality. Secondly we argue that people are complex tapestries of strengths and weaknesses, and what is a strength in one situation can be a weakness in another.

3. lastly, what is required to build a leadership community. We will focus on new and innovative approaches to leadership talent-spotting and leadership development techniques.

Book outline

In this book we address a number of themes that touch upon building a leadership community. We have also asked a number of guest authors to provide us with some of their views and experiences. The structure of the book is shown below.

- **Chapter 2: The new leadership landscape.** Too often leadership development initiatives are focused on a set of loosely defined or generic competencies and leadership styles that should be developed, without a clear link to the organisation-specific leadership requirements, brand behaviours and capabilities and competencies required for successful execution of the organisation's strategy. This missing link in leadership development can be described as the "requisite leadership landscape". We define "leadership community" as the nature, dynamics and evolution of a leadership grouping. The leadership community has its own ideology, brand, beliefs, value set and code of practice. In this chapter we also unpack the journey to building a leadership community.

- **Chapter 3: Corporate leadership community.** The quality of the leadership community of an organisation forms the leadership capital of an organisation. It thus critical that the make-up, dynamics and evolution of leadership communities are clearly understood and managed. We also explore how leadership communities can combat toxic leadership.

- **Chapter 4: Leaders are people too.** This chapter explores the human nature of leaders. We argue here that people are not always rational and that leadership development should not only be seen as "closing the gap".

- **Chapter 5: Creating leadership community-enabling conditions.** This chapter is based on extensive research on how to create enabling conditions to build the leadership community. It specifically highlights the role of the HR department, while making it clear that leadership capacity-building is not the responsibility of HR alone.

- **Chapter 6: Spotting leadership talent.** It is so easy to get the leadership talent identification thing wrong. Spotting leadership talent is a minefield as it is cluttered with our own perceptions and biases around what we think good leadership means. In this chapter we try to make some sense of identifying leadership talent. We also explain that leadership talent means different things at different levels of the organisation.

- **Chapter 7: New leadership development approaches.** In this chapter we explore some principles of leadership development and some thoughts on what works and doesn't work. Developing leadership community is about developing leadership at all levels of the organisation – it's not about only considering the needs of a few or of the individual. This also implies that the responsibility for development moves away from the organisation to the individual. We also explore some of the key future leadership development trends and practices.

- **Chapter 8: Not all that is measured counts**. Whilst there may be some broad consensus on how the "value" of leadership development can be calculated, there is significantly less clarity and consensus on how the business benefits of leadership itself can be determined. In this chapter we unpack the key principles that should inform the measurement of the benefits realised through leadership development processes and interventions.

- **Chapter 9: From dream to action**. In this final chapter we share some lessons learnt and hopefully provide you with some practical applications for your own organisation.

Despite the practical nature of this book, it does not give a simple "how to" recipe. It's also an attempt to reflect on leadership and sometimes have uncomfortable conversations about leadership and building leadership in organisations. Given the global shortage of leadership talent, it has become critically important that organisations translate the leadership brand into organisation-wide leadership capacity. Clearly, as with all other strategic imperatives, it is also important that the organisation takes a perspective on the impact that leadership capacity-building processes have on a broad range of business performance expectations and metrics.

Chapter 2

The new leadership landscape

Anton Verwey

Contributing author: Charles du Toit

❄

"The only thing we know about the future is that it is going to be different."
– Peter Drucker

"The illiterate of the 21st century will not be those who cannot read and write, but those who cannot learn, unlearn, and relearn." **– Alvin Toffler**

As mentioned in the previous chapter, the context within which leadership takes place has changed over the centuries and is changing again. This chapter (which is more scientific in its nature than the others) explores the changing leadership landscape to create a thinking framework for the rest of the book. To achieve this objective, this chapter defines leadership landscape, discusses its evolution, describes what we see as the new leadership landscape and then highlights some implications for leadership in organisations.

What is leadership landscape?

The use of term "landscape" is a very deliberate one. Any landscape one looks at has a number of dimensions in terms of which it may be described, such as geography, weather, fauna and flora, and so forth. Similarly, the leadership landscape of an organisation may also be described in a number of dimensions. One such description is provided in figure 2.1.

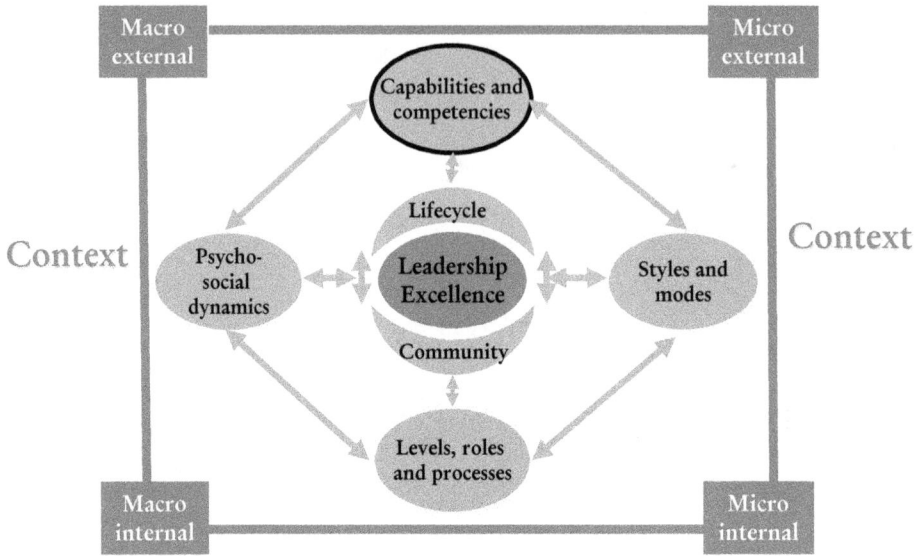

Figure 2.1. Leadership landscape[2]

As can be seen from figure 2.1, the key dimensions along which a leadership landscape may be viewed include the following:

- the context within which leadership is exercised (the macro and micro internal and external environments)

- leadership capabilities and competencies (capability is the ability to generate, prefer and demonstrate appropriate work-type specific complexity, values, activities, perceptions, judgement, interpersonal qualities, problem-solving etcetera. Competence is the ability to demonstrate work-type specific functional business and leadership competencies. Competency is typically described as comprising knowledge, skills and attitudes.)

- leadership styles and modes: leadership style focuses on the degree of empowerment (or freedom) leadership gives stakeholders, for example telling vs co-determination. Modes are the manner in which leadership exercises its influence, for example through an inspiring vision and meaning-giving values.

- leadership levels, roles and processes (the coherent set of actions undertaken by leadership; for example the processes leaders engage in to get employees to achieve organisational goals can include enabling people to perform, mobilising employees for action, empowering employees to meet goals etc)

- leadership psycho-social dynamics (the personal, interpersonal, team and organisational dynamics within the organisation). They are related to aspects such as ethics, power and influence.

- leadership lifecycle (the emergence, manifestation and demise of leadership over time). The leadership lifecycle is the stages leadership passes through, with their associated transitions (for example from one level of work to the next) in the organisation.

- leadership community (the nature, dynamics and evolution of a leadership grouping). The leadership group of an organisation forms a community of practice with its own ideology, brand, beliefs, value set and code of practice. Associated with the leadership community is a certain leadership culture and climate: the interpersonal, team and organisation-wide dynamics amongst the organisation's leadership. The quality of the leadership community of an organisation forms the leadership capital of an organisation. It is thus critical that the make-up, dynamics and evolution of leadership communities are clearly understood and managed.

All of these in combination allow us to express a view on the degree to which the organisation has leadership excellence or not.

The second point to be made is that the leadership landscape (similar to any other landscape) consists of a number of observable features, but also has some less obvious characteristics. Using the dimensions of landscape discussed above, table 2.1 illustrates some of these features. This table is not meant to be a complete list, but simply to stimulate some thoughts in the reader.

Table 2.1 Leadership landscape features

Dimension	Observable features	Hidden characteristics[5]
Context	industry type, market positioning	shifts in stakeholder expectations
Capabilities and competencies	performance against measurable expectations	performance expectations at lower levels of the organisation
Styles and modes	observable individual behaviour	motives and intent
Levels, roles and processes	ability to generate requisite complexity	work compression at lower levels
Psycho-social dynamics	observable team behaviour	negative politicking and mistrust
Lifecycle	tenure and age distribution	wisdom and informal status
Community	public communication	private disagreements
Excellence	stakeholder feedback	independent advocacy

The third point to be made about the leadership landscape is that what you see depends entirely on where you stand. In the words of the famous Bette Midler song, "… from a distance, the earth looks blue and green …". What we see when we observe the leadership landscape of an organisation depends on, amongst other things:

- whether we are part of the organisation or observing from the outside

- our own worldviews, values and beliefs

- our own experiences

- our own positioning in terms of the dimensions of the leadership landscape[4]

In practical terms, this means that it is impossible to describe "the truth" about the leadership effectiveness of any organisation. There will be many perspectives, possibly all equally valid. However, the reality is that when a sufficient critical mass shares a perspective or perception, this becomes the truth about the leadership in the organisation.[5] If enough people share the perception that you have a high degree of leadership effectiveness, this positive perception will have positive consequences for your organisation. The converse is of course also true, and the evidence for both scenarios is found in numerous research articles and publications.

At this stage the reader will have one possible definition or description of "leadership landscape", and may also have developed some questions or perspectives on leadership in their own or other organisations. In the next section of this chapter, we explore the evolution of the leadership landscape.

The evolution of leadership landscape

In this section we explore the evolution of thinking about leadership landscape by revisiting very briefly the history of how our perspectives on work, workers and leadership have evolved over time.[6]

Perspectives on society

The way we think about work, employees and leadership is likely to be best understood in the context of the way society broadly operates. A key contention of this book is that there are shifts at a societal level that directly impact on how we think about leaders and leadership in organisations. Of course, shifts at a societal level are nothing new, and the following brief quotes illustrate this:

> Modern industry has established the world market. All old-established national industries have been destroyed. They are dislodged by new industries whose products are consumed

in every corner of the globe. In place of old wants, we find new wants, requiring for their satisfaction the products of different lands and climes ... All fixed, fast-frozen relations are swept away, all new-formed ones become antiquated before they can ossify.[7]

Civilization, I apprehend, is nearly synonymous with order. However much we may differ touching such matters as the distribution of property, the domestic relations, the law of inheritance and the like, most of us, I should suppose, would agree that without order civilization, as we understand it, cannot exist. Now, although the optimist contends that, since man cannot foresee the future, worry about the future is futile, and that everything, in the best possible of worlds, is inevitably for the best, I think it clear that within recent years an uneasy suspicion has come into being that the principle of authority has been dangerously impaired, and that the social system, if it is to cohere, must be reorganized.[8]

Humanity finds itself "midstride between an old and new era, and we have not yet found our way. We know the old no longer works, yet the new is not yet formed clearly enough to be believed. We are developing a new story and in the process of altering much of what we think, feel and do."[9]

Shifts at the societal level is therefore not something new, and something we suspect every generation is at least intuitively aware of. The shift in some of the most basic underlying premises of modern society is the result of two major forces:

- a cultural shift from separateness-thinking to whole-systems thinking and from an external authority to inner knowing, inner wisdom and inner authority

- a growing realisation that society in its present form does not work and is not sustainable in the long run

While paradigm shifts are most often driven by technology, ultimately the most important manifestations are social – increasing the level of social complexity and leading to profound changes in society to which the company (as the dominant institution of the industrial age) must adapt. "Humankind has the ability to continue filling space or gaps with improved technologies, but lacks the capacity to embrace the very thing he has created".[10] Drucker says "Technology itself matters less than the changes which it triggers in substance, content and focus".[11] Some of these changes are

- the increasing focus on wholeness in society (organisations are part of a bigger system)

- the impact of the social, economic and political environment on the organisation

- the importance of being able to permeate traditional organisational boundaries

- the multiple stakeholders of organisations

- the rise in importance of talented employees and their need for more meaningful work

- the explosion of information and the speed at which information is transported globally

In the next two subsections of this chapter we explore in more detail how, against the backdrop of societal shifts, our perspectives on work and leadership specifically have evolved.

Perspectives on work and workers

Prior to the Industrial Revolution, work was largely seen as an activity to be disdained, carried out by slaves and less respected citizens such as merchants and workers. In this period, the Protestant concept of economic individualism and Martin Luther's idea of a calling played a critical role in setting the cultural and ideological stage for the Industrial Revolution.[12] Significant technological discoveries that made it possible to mass-produce gave rise to the Industrial Revolution and the substitution of machine power for manpower. In the new organisation, commercial success was determined by economy of scale and the quest for growth in order to realise returns and productivity.[13]

The introduction of mass-production systems resulted in the pace of work being determined by machine capacity, and labour being organised according to function as opposed to trade. The need for cheap labour had a range of significant social impacts, including urbanisation, child and family labour, 12-hour workdays and extreme working conditions.[14] The continuing need to increase productivity gave rise to the scientific approach to work organisation.[15] Taylor describes the average worker as being prone to "soldiering" or loafing, and says the only way to ensure increased work performance was to apply a combination of scientific principles and incentives.[16] Dessler[17] observes that "intentionally or not, scientific management proponents left the impression that workers could be treated as 'givens in the system,' 'as little more than appendages to their machines'."

Due to the First World War, there was an increased focus on the creation of working conditions that would assist in improving productivity.[18] During this period, the modern organisational structure began to take shape. Henry Fayol popularised the theory of administration,[19] Mooney and Reily added the ideas of division of labour and chain of command, and Urwick and Guilck the elements of purpose, process, persons and place.[20] Bureaucracy was introduced by Max Weber to describe the pure form of organisation with a well-defined hierarchy, division of work, a system of rules and duties, procedures, the impersonality of interpersonal relations and employment based on technical competencies.[21]

The role of variables other than physical working conditions, and the control of worker output and behaviour, was identified in the Hawthorne studies.[22] Dessler states: "Changes in group norms, satisfaction, motivation and patterns of supervision had a greater impact on performance and productivity than organisational structure and authority systems."[23]

The Second World War had a significant impact on work practice. The manufacturing capacity of nations was focused on the consumer pull of the war effort, and therefore productivity was motivated by a higher societal goal than the enrichment of the owner. Organisations became more adaptable and authority decentralised. The ideas of democratic and participative leadership began to appear in management literature.[24]

In the period from 1960 to 1990, the job market became increasingly unstable and significant changes to work practices occurred. Most significant was an increasing awareness of human and social rights and equality.[25] Married women re-entered the labour market, there was a move beyond divisionism and strategic business units, and "total quality" or "performance excellence" were established.[26] Coupled with these factors, computerised decision-making, financial management systems and production control systems shifted accountability to lower levels of management. At the same time, however, senior management acquired increased oversight of employee performance through indicators.[27]

Due to the complexity of the information technology (IT) and production systems, the transfer of power from those possessing knowledge about how to organise work to those doing the work occurred and, to a degree, levelled the playing field in terms of the importance of leaders and followers.[28]

The present age, driven by the spectacular impact of advanced computer technology, the world-wide web and the resultant dramatic rise of globalisation, is characterised by an increasing focus on the role of the individual employee in the performance of an organisation. Other significant recent shifts include a move towards work-life balance; women and diversity;[29] total quality management, ISO standards, business excellence models and frameworks;[30] lean manufacturing/management;[31] ethics;[32] global sourcing[33] and the ageing population.[34] All of these developments place a higher degree of reliance on the role of the employee. This reliance seems destined to expand, as a number of significant changes to the workplace of the future are emerging:

- the movement towards a uniform leadership culture in organisations – a leadership brand[35]

- a move away from bureaucracy. Peters describes a future workplace away from the traditional American corporate model.[36]

- the rise of "best company" practices to attract, retain and motivate employee talent. "In the long run: Talent = Brand. Brand = Talent. Case closed."[37] Best employer organisations have taken a dramatically different view of how to manage, lead and retain people as key assets. Google is cited as a key example.

- the challenge of the talent pool[38] and talent management[39]

- a significant change in the workplace of the future due to advances in IT solutions. Geldenhuys[40] describes the age of cybersphere as the age beyond cyberspace, in which the internet is hugely advanced though the wide expansion of fibre-optic technology and almost limitless bandwidth. Some of the impacts of this on work are:

  o Products are able to communicate replenishment needs.

  o Information on everything is immediately available.

  o Creativity will become a prized competency and an area of competitive advantage.

  o Leaders have the ability to have more frequent "virtual" contact with followers.

  o There is more direct performance visibility.[41]

  o A virtual workspace has emerged.[42]

  o Social business initiatives, like intra-organisation Facebook, and the interplay between these systems and leadership, have emerged.[43]

  o There is an increasingly stronger focus on issues of work-life balance.[44]

In summary, looking back over the twentieth century, there has been a dramatic shift in the world of work. The labour-exploitive, machine-driven Industrial Revolution has gradually shifted, due to the complexity of technology, to a period of increasing awareness that the effective management and use of the human element of organisations leads to higher performance and productivity.

The view of the role of the employee, originally a simple input into the process as described in scientific management and the bureaucratic organisation, has changed. Through the influence of behavioural theory and participative management thinking, and the sheer force of technological change, the current, commonly held view is that "our people are our greatest asset." Furthermore, employees are now viewed as a source of continuous improvement and an integral competitive element in the productive process of work.

This shift in thinking about the importance and role of the human element in the workplace has had a profound impact on the thinking about workplace leadership.

Emerging work trends of the future appear to indicate that there will be an increasing focus on the human element and input in the workplace as a key competitive component.

Perspectives on leadership

Parallel to changes in the world of work, leadership practice and thinking in the workplace have evolved considerably since the Industrial Revolution. Prior to that event, many leadership styles and approaches may have existed, but two dominant themes characterised how leaders were identified. The first held that leaders had unique strengths, skills and abilities that helped them rise above others; the other, that the leader was anointed by a higher power.[45] Dessler[46] describes the latter as the exercise of predestination. The leadership style described by Machiavelli, writing in the sixteenth century, as cited in Kellerman, is that of forceful leadership. He held that "the only truly bad leadership was weak leadership."[47] Dessler observes that during the period prior to the Industrial Revolution, "a rigid, hierarchical chain of command was the norm and authority and communications emanated from the top."[48]

Shortly after the Industrial Revolution, the scientific management idea of identifying the ideal employee for a position was reflected in the focus on identifying the traits which made leaders great. Stoghill[49] consolidates the results of a significant number of these studies, concluding that excellent leaders differed from average leaders in the traits of intelligence, alertness, insight, responsibility, initiative, persistence, self-confidence and sociability.

The Hawthorn studies, Elton Mayo and the humanistic movement introduced the idea that individuals operate most effectively when their needs are satisfied and that significant power within organisations exists at the level of interpersonal relationships.[50]

This resulted in leadership–employee relations becoming increasingly important in the quest for higher performance.[51] The differentiation between the new emerging theoretical approach to employees and workplace leadership and the traditional approach was described by McGregor, who argued that modern management needed to change its assumption about employees and tap into the real potential of the workforce. McGregor[52] calls the two approaches Theory X and Theory Y. Theory X embodies the traditional view that employees are largely motivated by lower-level needs and that they require close supervision. In contrast, McGregor proposes that people have much greater potential, as well as the creativity and capacity to be self-directed. Unleashing this potential, which he termed Theory Y, was the essential task of management.[53]

Two major shifts in leadership theory occurred during the period between 1950 and 1970. Firstly, a shift occurred from a traits approach to a leadership skills approach.

This shift was grounded in the idea that, as opposed to being inborn traits, leadership skills can be taught. These theories focused on the nature of the technical, human and conceptual skills of leadership. Secondly, it was recognised that effective leadership involves matching leadership behaviours and strategies to particular situational contexts. This approach is commonly termed "contingency theory".[54] Situational leadership theory, a popular contingency leadership approach, was first suggested by Redding in 1967 and further refined in 1969 by Hersey and Blanchard.[55] They differentiate between situational activities (high task focus or strong relationship focus), and different levels of employee ability and willingness. No one style is appropriate at all times and the effective leader is able to select the correct style for the specific circumstances.[56]

During the last quarter of the twentieth century, the importance of leadership in business became an increasing focus in the United States of America. Kellerman[57] ascribes this development to the fact that American companies faced new challenges and changes: "The control of oil by OPEC, foreign competition (especially from Japan), inflation and regulation disturbed the smooth workings of 'corporate machines' and threatened to overwhelm us."[58] An entire industry of literature and research into the quest for the secrets to successful organisational leadership emerged.[59] To a large degree, these theoretical approaches continue to add to the trait and contingency-or-context understanding of the practice of leadership within an organisation. Contributions include that of Stogdill,[60] who, in a survey of 163 trait theories, found that both personality and situational factors were determinants of leadership.

Recently, leadership theory shifted focus from developing an understanding of leadership traits and contextual or contingency theories, to a focus on the psychological contract between the leader and the follower, the leadership role of assisting employees to cope with change, and the evolving nature of this relationship as a way to incrementally improve individual growth and resultant organisational performance. Von Eck and Verwey[61] identify five schools of leadership:

- transactional leadership, in which leaders motivate followers towards established goals

- transformational leadership, which focuses on developing "an appealing vision of the future" and appeals to the intrinsic motivation of the follower

- charismatic leadership, which relates to the ability to inspire people towards a goal

- servant leadership, which places service and the development of the follower at the core

- transcendental leadership, which refers to leaders who relate to the "spirituality that compels leaders to look beyond their own egos and to be more concerned about an internal development that transcends realities as defined by the environment"[62]

The transactional leadership approach was first expressed in the leader-member exchange theory (LMX), which appeared in the 1975 work of Dasereau, Green and Haga.[63] They describe "leadership as a process that is centred on the interactions between leaders and followers".[64] The underlying thinking in LMX theory is that leaders exchange rewards for employees' compliance, a concept based on bureaucratic authority and a leader's legitimacy within an organisation,[65] especially during times of organisational change.[66] This approach is typified by a low level of shared governance.[67]

Transformational leadership (including charismatic leadership) is an approach that has received significant focus since the early 1980s. As opposed to the transactional leader, who provides rewards for support (a transaction), the transformational leader engages with others and creates a connection that raises the level of motivation and morality in both the leader and the follower.[68] Northhouse and Stone and Patterson[69] describe transformational leaders as individuals who are seen as outstanding leaders across many contexts, are extremely knowledgeable and trustworthy, are sensitive to follower needs and encouraging of follower growth and development. Gardiner[70] describes the transformational leader as one who "asks followers to transcend their own self-interests for the good of the group, organisation, or society; to consider their longer-term needs to develop themselves, rather than their needs of the moment; and to become more aware of what is really important."

Servant leadership is accredited by Stone and Patterson[71] to Robert Greenleaf. Greenleaf[72] described a servant leader as one who is motivated by the needs of his or her followers rather than self-interest. The servant leader is motivated first and foremost by a desire to further the development of the follower[73] and build a "shared culture".[74] Melchar and Bosco[75] found that, in organisations in which senior-level leaders displayed servant leadership, the servant leadership at all levels of the organisation was enhanced.

Von Eck and Verwey[76] describe transcendental leadership as incorporating the styles of transactional, transformational and servant leadership. A transcendental leadership view includes cognition, emotional intelligence and spiritual intelligence. Collins[77] refers to a similar higher-level leadership, which he terms a Level 5 leadership model. Von Eck[78] found that transcendental leadership competencies are required in all changing environments. This leadership style sees the employees and their wellbeing as the central focus of an organisation. Gardiner observes that "Transcendent leadership offers us a metaphor to help us move more closely to a world where human talents and energies will be maximised for the betterment of all – personally, organisationally, and globally."[79]

The role that leaders play in an increasingly changing world is a central theme in modern leadership theory. Van der Merwe and Verwey[80] describe how a new era of uncertainty and rapid change has resulted in increasing complexity, and that this change demands a different set of leader competencies to the traditional. This dynamic is described as follows: "Leaders need to be the rock of Gibraltar on rollerblades".[81]

In the modern world, more than just "coping with our environment and reacting to it ... modern leaders need a second attention ... an enduring and heightened sense of awareness"; the "illusion of control" is flawed and leaders need to be able to cope with a landscape of competing values".[82] "One function of the competing values framework is to help leaders find ways to capitalise on the strengths of opposite quadrants and to think in ways that give rise to transformational thinking."[83] Van der Merwe[84] describes a range of meta-competencies for the leaders of the future. These competencies are based on the future work of leaders being designing and developing the purpose of the organisation, making sense of what is happening, and governance for survival.

These studies, while presenting different ideas of leadership, all support a leadership approach that is focused on the employee and places the responsibility on the leader, within the changing world of work, to create an environment in which the employee thrives.

This is the specific objective of positive organisational scholarship (POS), an offshoot of positivist psychology, which draws on theory from the full spectrum of sciences that study organisational behaviour.[85] The use of the term "positive" in POS, as a form of positivism, focuses on affirmative and generative states and dynamic approaches to organisational behaviour, and the term "scholarship" emphasises the scientific research basis of the approach.[86] Luthans[87] uses a similar term, "positive organisational behavior," to describe "the study and application of positively oriented human resource strengths and psychological capacities that can be measured, developed, and effectively managed for performance improvement in today's workplace." He names "confidence (or self-efficacy), hope, optimism, subjective well-being (or happiness), and emotional intelligence" as the psychological capabilities that meet the positive organisational behaviour criteria. These variables are called PsyCap in POS terminology and have been shown to generally relate to desirable workplace outcomes.[88] They are indicators of the future direction of leadership to enhance organisational performances.[89]

While cautioning against excessive focus on either positive or negative organisational behaviour, Bright, Alzola, Stansbury and Stavros[90] recognise that there is a natural tendency in organisations to focus on the negative. Cameron concludes that the "empirical evidence is clear that when positive factors are given greater emphasis than negative factors, human beings tend toward positive change."[91]

POS is of specific relevance to the study of leadership. Cameron describes positive leadership as a means of promoting positive organisational outcomes, such as thriving at work, interpersonal flourishing, virtuous behaviours, positive emotions and energising networks. Such leadership is rare but specifically relevant in the current world of work.[92] Cameron and Lavine[93] contrast the difference between conventional leadership principles and abundance (positive) leadership principles, as seen in table 2.2.

Table 2.2 Conventional leadership principles compared with abundance leadership principles

Conventional principles	Abundance principles
General leadership principles	
<ul><li>problem-solving and deficit gaps</li><li>a single heroic leader</li><li>one leader from beginning to end</li><li>congruence and consistency</li></ul>	<ul><li>virtuousness and abundance gaps</li><li>multiple leaders playing multiple roles</li><li>a continuity of leaders</li><li>paradox and contradiction</li></ul>
Principles related to visionary and symbolic leadership	
<ul><li>left-brain, visions – logical, rational and sensible – with SMART goals</li><li>consistency, stability and predictability</li><li>personal benefits and advantages</li><li>organisations absorb the risks of failure and benefits of success</li></ul>	<ul><li>right-brain, visions – symbolic, emotional and meaningful – with profound purpose</li><li>revolution and positive deviance</li><li>meaningfulness beyond personal benefits</li><li>employees share the risks of failure and rewards of success</li></ul>
Principles related to careful, clear and controlled leadership	
<ul><li>downsizing at the expense of people</li><li>commitments and priorities based on environmental demands</li><li>managing the contractor, attaching resources to performance</li><li>ultimate responsibility and accountability for measurable success at the top</li><li>adaptability and addressing work challenges as they arise</li></ul>	<ul><li>downsizing for the benefit of people</li><li>unalterable commitments and integrity at all costs</li><li>managing the contract and ensuring stable funding</li><li>everyone responsible and accountable for measurable success, including workers, managers, regulators, community, organisation and funders</li><li>engaging only in value-added activities</li></ul>
Principles related to collaborative, engaging and participative leadership	
<ul><li>building on reinforcing the current culture</li><li>decision-making and leadership at the top</li><li>need-to-know information sharing and physical separation</li><li>long-term employment, personal relations and the use of specialists</li></ul>	<ul><li>introducing challenges that the culture cannot address</li><li>employee and union partnerships in planning, decision-making, training, evaluation and discipline</li><li>early, frequent and abundant information-sharing with co-location</li><li>long-term employability, professional relations and retraining</li></ul>

Principles related to rigorous, uncompromising and results-oriented leadership	
• managing the media • keeping adversaries at a distance and using protective political strategies • clear, stable performance targets that meet standards coming from the top • organisational financial benefit from outstanding success	• openness with the media early and often • making adversaries stakeholders, building relationships and using positive political strategies • escalating performance, virtuousness and positive deviance targets from multiple sources • financial generosity and benevolence with employees

Cameron[94] proposes that there are four leadership strategies that will produce positive and flourishing outcomes in organisations: a positive climate, positive relationships, positive communication and positive meaning. These POS leadership strategies are predicted to have a significant impact on future leadership training and development.[95] Current research is emerging on the applications of positive leadership, including the link between emotional intelligence and positive leadership styles,[96] transformational leadership,[97] servant leadership styles[98] and the positive group affect spiral.[99]

Authentic leadership is a positivistic leadership focus,[100] which has emerged out of the economic crises of the past few years. Luthans and Youssef[101] describe authentic leadership as a pattern of transparent, ethical leader behaviour that encourages openness to input and information. In authentic leadership, there is consistency with action and virtue over external influence.[102] Spitzmuller and Ilies[103] found that authentic leaders are generally transformational, depending on the situational context and the followers. Walumbwa et al[104] suggest that "by combining authentic, ethical, and transformational leadership into our training regimens, we may be able to provide some of the strongest positive impacts on long-term motivation and sustaining high levels of performance."

Drath, McCauley, Palus, Van Velsor, O'Connor and McGuire[105] argue that traditional leadership models are based on the relationships between the leader, the follower and their shared goals, but are now shifting as these relationships become increasingly collaborative. They argue for a new ontology for leadership in which "to practice leadership would no longer necessarily involve leaders, followers, and their shared goals but would necessarily involve the production of direction, alignment, and commitment (which may or may not involve leaders and followers)".[106] Avery[107] describes a continuum from traditional to organic leadership paradigms, differentiating four major paradigms:

- a classical paradigm in which the leader has positional power and is accountable for results. Followers largely carry out instructions with limited scope for internal dialogue. This paradigm is largely top-down.

- transactional leadership, in which the leader's responsibilities are "managing the whole internal and external environment to influence followers, recognising their needs and wants and clarifying how it is possible to meet this complexity through negotiated rewards and agreements system"[108]

- visionary, transformational or charismatic leadership. In this paradigm, there is an emotional bond between the leader and follower which creates space for a collaborative dialogue towards a vision of organisational outcome.

- organic leadership, in which there is no formal distinction between leader and follower, but rather teams in which roles are based not on positional power but on knowledge

Organic leadership, which allows people with different degrees of expertise on current issues to emerge and be accepted by the group as leaders, is described by Jing and Avery.[109] Rok[110] describes the organic leader as temporal, a servant or facilitator, self-controlled and organised, sharing vision and values, with a clear sense of purpose and autonomy within a particular context.

Important in the emergence of the concept "leadership brand" is the development of the notion that leadership exists within organisations, beyond individual or team contexts.

Lichtenstein, Uhl-bien, Marion, Seers, Orton and Schreiber[111] propose that research into the leadership within an organisation requires an understanding of the complexity of the leadership dynamic, which "transcends the capabilities of individuals alone; it is the product of interaction, tension, and exchange rules governing changes in perceptions and understanding." They call this approach "complexity leadership theory". Hazy, Goldstein and Lichtenstein[112] describe leadership as the dynamic that emerges across groups of people through interaction and as "a *systemic* event rather than as a personal attribute."[113] In complexity leadership theory, leadership is "not merely the influential act of an individual or individuals but rather is embedded in a complex interplay of numerous interacting forces".[114] In a review of recent literature on leadership, Avolio, Walumbwa and Weber[115] comment that the theory of leadership needs to develop beyond conceptual discussions.

The collective dimension of leadership is described by Ulrich and Smallwood,[116] who introduce the idea of a leadership brand. They describe the importance of organisations creating a distinguishable brand of leadership which describes the authentic employee experience of the organisations' collective leadership. This "brand" has significant value for the organisation and its stakeholders. Younger and Smallwood[117] describe a leadership brand in the context of an organisation being branded because of the organisation's reputation as a developer of talent and its view of employee development as a strategic issue.

Summary

In summary, the shift in organisational thinking about leadership issues over the past 100 years has brought about a complete transformation. The authoritarian leadership approach of the Industrial Revolution, in which the central theme was the identification of "great man" traits, has evolved across the centuries to the quest for transcendental, authentic servant leaders and corporate leadership brands. This is illustrated in figure 2.2.

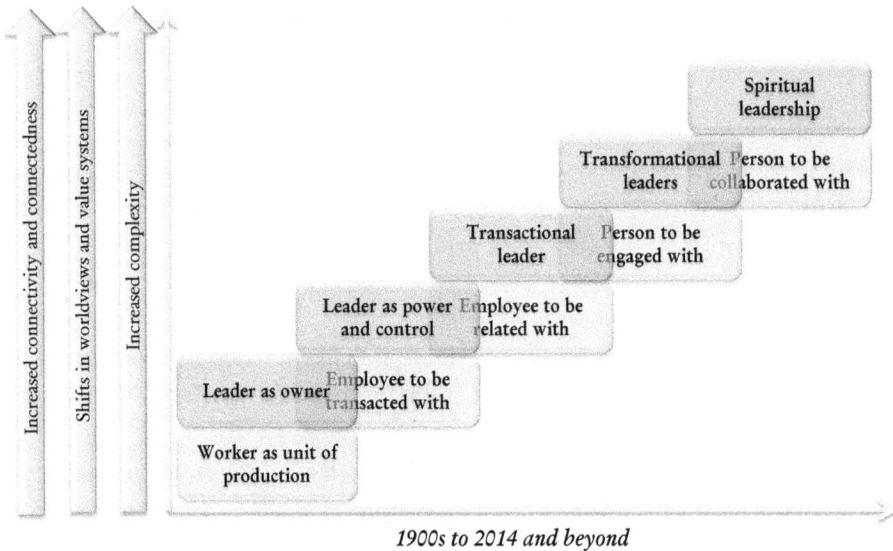

Figure 2.2 The philosophical shift in leadership theory

With the shift in thinking around the importance of the role of the human element in the workplace and the shift in leadership thinking towards employee-centred leadership, a more contextual view of leadership, namely leadership brand, has emerged. It is precisely this shift towards leadership brand that has at least two consequences of key importance to this book, namely:

- We are less concerned about "the leader" and much more concerned about leadership excellence across the organisation.

- We are of the view that a sustainable leadership brand only becomes possible through the deliberate creation and maintenance of a leadership community.

How might this shift in philosophical (and practical!) definitions of leaders and leadership change our perspectives on the leadership landscape? In the next section of this chapter, the leadership landscape as defined in What is Leadership Landscape on page 9 is revisited to reflect on some key changes in dynamics.

The new leadership landscape

Given the initial definition and description of leadership landscape and the story of how our thinking about leaders and leadership has evolved over time, as discussed in the preceding sections of this chapter, we now attempt to bring these together into a perspective on what may be called a "new" leadership landscape.

Two key issues are addressed in this section of this chapter, namely 1) the interplay and dynamics between complexity of work and 2) the driving forces behind (or underneath) the shifts in this dynamic.

Complexity and values

In our view, there are at least two issues related to leadership (and leadership community) of organisations that should be considered. Specifically, the interplay between these may provide interesting perspectives on the dynamics that play out in real life.

Levels of work

Stratified Systems Theory (SST) is in our view a very useful framework in which to understand the inherent complexity of work. Stratified systems theory is

> primarily a theory of organisational structure in relation to the competitiveness required for survival in a world environment. Second, it is a theory of managerial performance requirements derived from that structure and of managerial capability necessary to deal with the performance requirements".[118]

The characteristics of the seven levels of complexity are illustrated in table 2.3.[119]

Table 2.3 Levels of work

Level	Theme	Description	Timespan of discretion
I	Quality	making or doing something that can be fully specified beforehand, has a concrete or direct output and an immediate impact on viability	up to 3 months
II	Service	demonstrating the purpose of organisations in response to particular situations, cases and customers	up to one year

Level	Theme	Description	Timespan of discretion
III	Practice	maintaining various ways in which purpose is realised in provision of services and the production of goods – improving practice	up to 2 years
IV	Development	managing the relationship between strategic intent and the means – develop new methods	up to 5 years
V	Strategic intent	ensuring the external and internal wellbeing of the organisation – representing the organisation to the external socio-economic context	up to 10 years
VI	Corporate citizenship	reading within economic, political, social, technological and religious contexts	15 or 20 years
VII	Corporate prescience	sustaining viability for future generations	more than 20 years

Jaques[120] also links this functional responsibility back to the individual's ability to cope with levels of complexity with reference to "levels of work". Jaques includes time horizon and complexity of information as individual managing capabilities within an organisation reflecting the level of work being performed. A key issue in SST is therefore that human capability needs to match the requirements of the inherent level of complexity of the work (or system).

While there is a significant amount of research and writing on the topic of the capability of individuals to generate the complexity required by the work they are accountable for, in our view an equally important element of human capability is the underlying values system.

Spiral dynamics

Spiral dynamics argues that human nature is not fixed: humans are able, when forced by life conditions, to adapt to their environment by constructing new, more complex, conceptual models of the world that allow them to handle the new problems. Each new model transcends and includes all previous models. According to Beck and Cowan,[121] these conceptual models are organised around so-called vMemes (pronounced "v memes"): systems of core values or collective intelligences, applicable to both individuals and entire cultures.

In spiral dynamics, the term vMeme refers to a core value system, acting as an organising principle, which expresses itself through memes (self-propagating ideas, habits or cultural practices). The lower-case letter v indicates these are not basic memes but value systems that include them. The colours act as reminders of the life conditions and mind capacities of each system and alternate between cool and warm colours as a part of the model. Within the model, individuals and cultures do not fall clearly in any single category (colour).

A review of the vMemes also shows that these alternate between a focus on self-interest and one on concern for others. Each person/culture embodies a mixture of the value patterns, with varying degrees of intensity in each. Spiral dynamics claims not to be a linear or hierarchical model, although this assertion has been contested.

The characteristics of the vMemes are illustrated in table 2.4.

Table 2.4 Spiral dynamics

vMeme	Self-interest	Concern for others
Turquoise Holistic		• blending and harmonising a strong collective of individuals • focus on the good of all living entities as integrated systems • expanded use of human brain/mind tools and competencies • self is part of a larger, conscious, spiritual whole that also serves the self • global (and whole-spiral!) networking seen as routine • acts for minimalist living so less actually is more
Yellow Systemic	• accept the inevitability of nature's flows and forms; focus on functionality, competence, flexibility and spontaneity; find natural mix of conflicting "truths" and "uncertainties" • discover personal freedom without harm to others or excesses of self-interest; demand integrative and open systems	

vMeme	Self-interest	Concern for others
Green Relativistic		• explore the inner beings of self and others • promote a sense of community and unity • share society's resources among all • liberate humans from greed and dogma • reach decisions through consensus • refresh spirituality and bring harmony
Orange Strategic	• strive for autonomy and independence • seek out "the good life" and material abundance • progress by searching out the best solutions • enhance living for many through science and technology • play to win and enjoy competition • learning through tried-and-true experience	
Blue Purposeful		• find meaning and purpose in living • sacrifice self to the way for deferred reward • bring order and stability to all things • control impulsivity and respond to guilt • enforce principles of righteous living
Red Egocentric	• in a world of haves and have-nots, it's good to be a have • avoid shame, defend reputation, be respected • gratify impulses and sense immediately • fight remorselessly and without guilt to break constraints • don't worry about consequences that may not come	

vMeme	Self-interest	Concern for others
Purple Clannish		• obey desires of the mystical spirit beings • show allegiance to elders, custom, clan • preserve sacred places, objects, rituals • bond together to endure and find safety
Beige Instinctive	• automatic, autistic, reflexive • centres around satisfaction • driven by deep brain programmes, instincts and genetics • minimal impact on or control over environment	

According to spiral dynamics, there are infinite stages of progress and regression over time, dependent upon the life circumstances of the person or culture, which are constantly in flux. Attaining higher stages of development is not synonymous with attaining a "better" or "more correct" value system. All stages co-exist in both healthy and unhealthy states, meaning any stage of development can lead to undesirable outcomes with respect to the health of the human and social environment.

SST and spiral dynamics in interaction

The above two sets of theory become really interesting from the perspective of leadership community when we ask whether or not there is a relationship between complexity (SST) on the one hand and value systems (vMeme) on the other hand. Some specific questions that could be posed include:

• What happens to our ability to generate complexity if our values are primarily based on self-interest?

• What happens when personal value systems do not align with the expectation of the larger leadership community?

Our attempt to respond to these questions is summarised in figure 2.3.

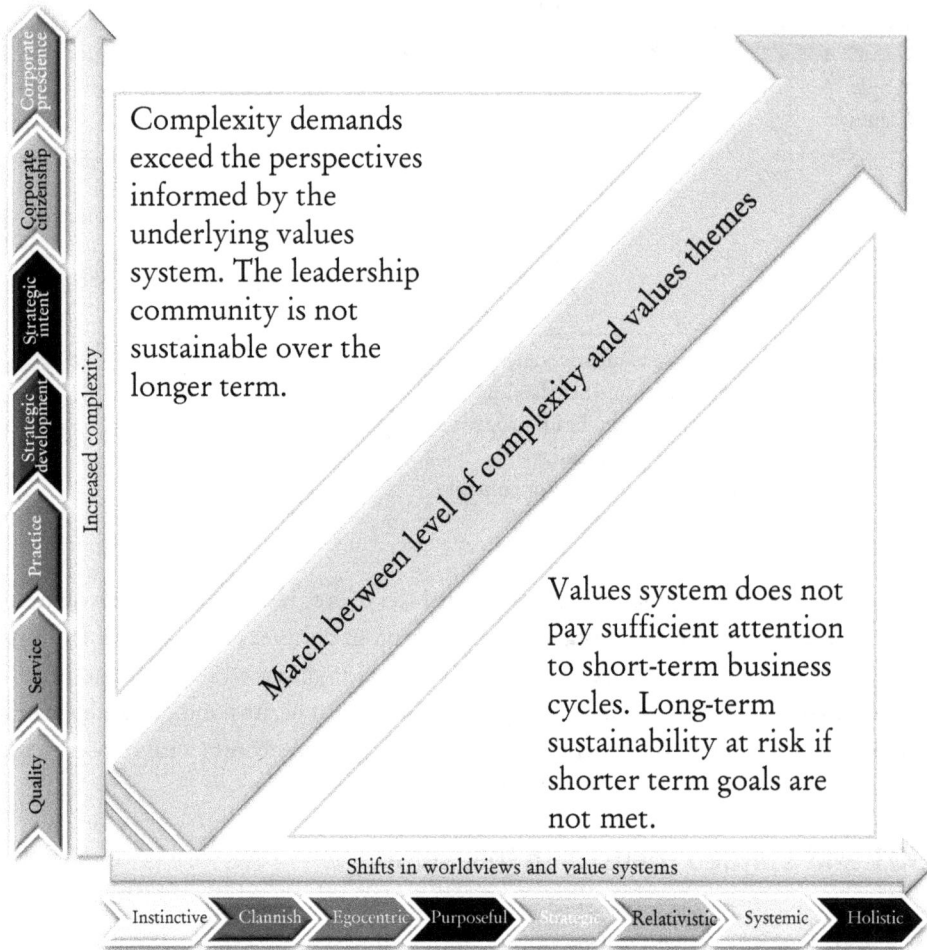

Complexity demands exceed the perspectives informed by the underlying values system. The leadership community is not sustainable over the longer term.

Match between level of complexity and values themes

Values system does not pay sufficient attention to short-term business cycles. Long-term sustainability at risk if shorter term goals are not met.

Increased complexity

Shifts in worldviews and value systems

Corporate prescience | Corporate citizenship | Strategic intent | Strategic development | Practice | Service | Quality

Instinctive | Clannish | Egocentric | Purposeful | Strategic | Relativistic | Systemic | Holistic

Figure 2.3 Level of complexity and values themes

In simple terms, our view is therefore that misalignment between personal values (and those of the leadership community) and the inherent complexity of work poses a risk to the leadership community as well as the organisation(s) they are members of. In our own work, we have seen the devastating effects of this on employee engagement and commitment, client satisfaction and corporate reputation.

Summary

In this section we described the possible interaction between levels of work complexity and values systems, and in the next section we explore how this interaction may inform our thinking about some of the driving forces behind shifts in perspectives on leadership landscape.

Driving forces

In considering what the driving forces behind these shifts in leadership landscape may be, a useful thinking framework is the well-known Porter model[122] that attempts to describe and understand our organisational environment by looking at the following dimensions:

- political
- economic
- social
- technological
- legislative
- environmental

Given the primary focus of this chapter, we focus particularly on how these impact on the more "human" aspects of leadership. Of course, this is not meant to be a complete or definitive analysis, but will hopefully be sufficient to stimulate thinking and questioning by the reader. Refer to table 2.5.

Table 2.5 PESTLE and leadership landscape

Dimension	PESTLE impacts
Context	Through technological advances, predominantly travel and mass communication (including the internet), the notion of boundaries has shifted quite dramatically. The idea of being an international (if not global) company is not a strange one, bringing with it the challenge of leading across cultural boundaries as much as geographic ones. Increasingly, organisations have to accept that they are simply part of a network of networks, and rarely if ever are they at the centre of any of these.
Capabilities and competencies	A recent research study suggested that the current young generation is the first in the history of humankind that will be less educated than the previous generation. A South African university found that of more than 3 000 applications for first-year graduate studies, only 200 prospective students qualified for admission based on entry-level requirements. These are the individuals that will lead your organisation in the not-too-distant future!

Styles and modes	The key shift in leadership styles and modes seems to be the move from transactional/transformational leadership towards transcendental or spiritual leadership. At the heart of this lies a very different perspective or view of the nature of the relationship between organisation and environment, and leadership and followership.
Levels, roles and processes	The key issue is without a doubt the simultaneous increase in the complexity of organisations and a fundamental shift in values. For the former, a common term used is "boundary-less collaboration", while for the latter the notion of "democratised connectedness" seems to be a trend. The inevitable consequences of these are a reduced ability to rely on lessons from the past and an increased need to exercise sound judgement.[123]
Psycho-social dynamics	The one issue that seems to be common almost globally is the expression of a lack of trust in formal authority. Civil unrest and disobedience are commonplace throughout the world. Organisational leaders often express concern about the "culture of entitlement". The dynamics between wise elders, good citizens and young Turks is under pressure as never before.[124]
Lifecycle	China and Africa have a very young and growing population, while many European countries have a progressively older and smaller population. This creates some interesting challenges for organisations and their future leadership, especially when viewed in parallel with the comments made above about capabilities and competencies.
Community	Traditionally, it was fairly easy to define a specific community. With people moving across the globe, this idea is suddenly less clear. Hundreds of thousands of South Africans live and work in countries such as Australia, New Zealand and the United Kingdom. Millions of Zimbabweans, Nigerians, Malawians and Congolese have moved to South Africa. A similar migration has happened from Eastern to Western Europe. Suddenly, the notion of community and community membership is no longer simple. Similarly, with organisations really being networks of networks, how do we create a "community" with identifiable boundaries, characteristics and meaning to its members?
Excellence	Given all of the preceding, our perspectives on what leadership excellence is and how it may be evidenced really need some significant rethinking. Clearly though, we cannot assume that what worked up to now will continue to do so into the future.

A new leadership landscape

Given the above, our own conclusions and interpretation of how the leadership landscape has shifted are summarised in figure 2.4 and table 2.6.

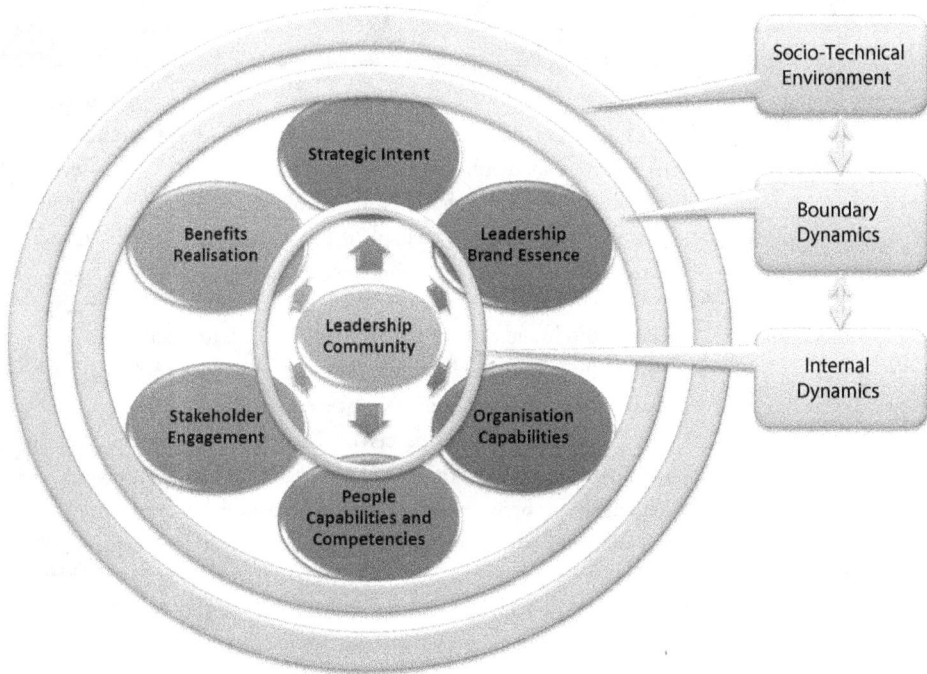

Figure 2.4 A new leadership landscape

Table 2.6 A new leadership landscape

Landscape dimension	Description
Socio-technical environment	Rather than refer to the typical PESTLE framework, we are of the view that organisations are generally very aware of the technical (economic, legislative, technology and environment) aspects, but significantly less aware of the political and social dimensions of the world around them. In this context, we do not of course mean national or even international formal politics, but the more fundamental shifts related to perspectives on power and influence.
Boundary dynamics	We have made the point already that organisations are in effect part of very complex networks of networks. The awareness of the constantly shifting boundary dynamics becomes a key aspect of the ability to collaborate and compete simultaneously. In our view it is in this space that the organisation can make or break its systemic integrity.

Landscape dimension	Description
Strategic intent	Given the above two dimensions, strategic intent becomes much more than the articulation of a desired competitive positioning. At a very fundamental level it becomes a statement of purpose. A simplistic "serving of shareholder interests" is simply not enough; organisations must also be explicit about their purpose or value to various stakeholders, including broader society.
Leadership brand essence	Leadership brand essence has two sides to it. Externally, it is essentially our corporate reputation, that is how our boundary partners view us based on their interaction with us over time. Internally, it is our perceived culture, that is how our members (employees) think and feel about us (and themselves!). Misalignment between these two has devastating consequences for the ability of our organisation to deliver on its stated purpose.
Organisation capabilities	A key role of leadership at all levels is to create and maintain the requisite capability to consistently deliver on purpose **and** the leadership brand essence. This is about our technologies, processes, infrastructure, business and operating models and so forth. Even more important, it is also about our social fabric.
People capabilities and competencies	It is only in the context of clear purpose, a defined leadership brand and the requisite organisational capabilities that we can deliberately attract, develop and retain people with the capabilities and competencies that will allow us to achieve our goals and them to achieve theirs. A fundamental point of departure here is that true talent joins us (and stays with us) by **their** choice.
Stakeholder engagement	Ideally, we would have liked to find a different word for "stakeholder" as it has become a real cliché. In our context, it really means everybody who believes they have a legitimate interest in what happens inside your organisation, as well as at the points of boundary dynamics. Of course these people include customers, shareholders, government, various interest groups and so forth. Increasingly though, we suspect that organisations will be confronted by expectations from stakeholders that they never knew existed.

Landscape dimension	Description
Benefits realisation	It should really come as no surprise that the benefits we deliver as organisations go beyond balanced scorecards, triple or quadruple bottom lines or other similar measures of performance. All of these make the implicit assumption that we have to make profit in order to realise the others.
Internal dynamics	The nature of the interplay between all the preceding dimensions creates what one may refer to as the internal dynamics of the organisation. However much we try to formalise structures, processes, roles and so forth, it appears that there is always an element of organisational reality that is unpredictable and occasionally even irrational. As individual leaders we are unlikely to be fully aware of it, and we definitely cannot control it.
Leadership community	In our view, leadership community has become the core of the leadership landscape of the organisation, at least seen from the perspective of the organisation itself. The constantly shifting internal and external dynamics and the implications of this for context, purpose and process require a point of stability. In our view, this point is leadership community. Of course, aspects such as leadership lifecycle, styles, modes and roles (see figure 2.1) are still relevant, but they need to be understood within a much broader and more dynamic context.

A comparison between the leadership landscape descriptions as set out in The New Leadership Landscape in figure 2.4 will show that there are a number of key differences:

- We are suggesting a much stronger relationship between social patterns and trends and the nature of leadership.

- We are strongly suggesting that the notion of "the leader" be supplemented with an equally strong focus on "leadership community":

  o The leadership of an organisation forms a community of practice with its own ideology, beliefs, value set and code of practice.

  o Associated with the leadership community is a certain leadership culture – the interpersonal, team and organisation-wide dynamics between and amongst the organisation's leadership.

Manfred Kets de Vries[125] writes:

> Although the ghost of the Great Man still haunts leadership studies, most of us have recognised by now that successful organisations are the product of distributive, collective, and complementary leadership. The first step in putting together such a team is to identify each member of the team's personality makeup and leadership style, so that strengths and competences can be matched to particular roles and challenges. Getting this match wrong can bring misery to all concerned and cause considerable damage.

Final remarks

This chapter explored the changing leadership landscape to create a thinking framework for the rest of the book. To achieve this objective, we defined leadership landscape, discussed its evolution, described what we see as the new leadership landscape and then highlighted some implications for leadership in organisations.

In the next chapter, we expand on the idea of leadership community by defining the construct, describing what it does for your business (ie why it matters), how it is created and maintained, and finally how its benefits may be determined.

Chapter 3

Leadership community

Anton Verwey

❄

"There is nothing wrong with creating greater shareholder value or making a profit in your company ... However there is something wrong when a Fortune 500 company doesn't consider that its primary mission should be to exist for the sake of others, and not just for the sake of others in their exclusive shareholder family, but for the sake of making this world to the least and the last a better place" —**Tony Baron**

A key issue in the preceding chapter is the notion of leadership versus "the leader", and the conditions that have evolved over time to create the need for a different and broader perspective on leadership community. Specific reference was made to the interplay between this requirement and the ability to generate higher-order complexity on the one hand and adopting an appropriate values set on the other.

In this chapter the objective is to explore leadership community in more detail. First we explore what the word "community" really means, then we define a leadership community, describe what it does for your business (ie why it matters), how it is created and maintained, and finally how its benefits may be determined.

Figure 3.1 shows that we are now paying specific attention to the very centre of the new leadership landscape as proposed in the preceding chapter (see also figure 2.3).

Figure 3.1 Focusing on leadership community

This chapter, in combination with chapter 2, also sets the stage for discussing in more detail some new perspectives on identifying (chapter 6) and nurturing and developing leadership talent (chapter 7).

What is community?

Before exploring leadership community in detail, it is appropriate to first define what precisely we mean by "community", as there may be very different (and valid) understandings of the concept.

The nature of community[126]

Like most things in the social sciences, "community" does not fit into a nice neat package. We cannot see a whole community, we cannot touch it, and we cannot directly experience it. More importantly, a community is not just the people who are in it. It is something that is beyond its very members. A "community" in some senses may not even have a physical location, but be demarcated by being a group of people with a common interest. It is a set of interactions and human behaviours that are not just actions, but actions based on shared expectations, values, beliefs and meanings between individuals. Community is a "cultural organism".

Characteristics of community

Table 3.1 describes the key characteristics of a community, and takes its descriptions of the characteristics predominantly from the perspective of formal organisations.

Table 3.1 Community characteristics

Characteristic	Description
A community has fuzzy boundaries.	When an identified community is a company, its boundaries appear at first to be very simple. That pattern of human interaction may be seen as consisting only of relationships between the members of that organisation. But the people in the organisation also interact with people outside the company, so the boundary of that company is not so precise.
Communities can be within communities.	Companies usually consist of different divisions, departments or functions, and may even have parts that are situated in different countries.
Communities move.	Furthermore, where technology is not based on local horticulture, the community residents may be physically mobile. They may be nomadic herders walking long distances with their cattle. They may be mobile fishing groups who move from time to time to where the fish are available. They may be hunters who move to follow the game.
Community is more than the sum of the parts.	The community has a life of its own which goes beyond the sum of the lives of all its residents. As a social organisation, a community is cultural (see Culture). That means it is a system of systems, and that it is composed of things that are learned rather than transmitted by genes and chromosomes. All the social or cultural elements of a community, from its technology to its shared beliefs, are transmitted and stored by symbols.
A community is a superorganic organism or system.	A community can be seen as something like an organism (ie it is organised; it has organs). It lives and functions even though its members come and go, are born or die. So, too, an individual human being is subject to a different set of forces than the community where he or she lives. A community then is a system – not an inorganic system like an engine, not an organic system like a tree, but a superorganic system built up of the learned ideas, expectations and behaviour of human beings.

Characteristic	Description
Communities are not homogenous.	Although a community is a cultural system (in that it transcends its individual persons) do not assume that a community is a harmonious unit. It isn't. It is full of factions, struggles and conflicts, based upon differences in gender, religion, access to wealth, ethnicity, class, educational level, income, ownership of capital, language and many other factors.

Since the notion of "community" is a social construct, it is important to understand the nature of "social". What, for example, is the "glue" that holds a community (or any social organisation) together? How can individuals be interdependent upon each other, even while they believe they are independent organisms? Do such beliefs, even if they are not accurate, serve some purpose in sustaining or supporting social organisation? While social scientists may disagree about the precise nature of those interconnections, all will agree that the basic characteristic of communities (and thus of the communities within a community) is that they are interconnected. A community, like other social institutions, is not merely a collection of individual people; it is a changing set of relationships, including the attitudes and behaviour of its members.

Community is learned

We mentioned above that a community is a cultural organism, and that it goes beyond those individual human beings that make it up. Culture consists of all those things, including the actions and beliefs that human beings learn, which make them human. Culture includes learned behaviour, and is stored and transmitted by symbols.

Culture is superorganic (and a community is cultural). Understanding the concept "superorganic" is important in understanding a community. Just as a tree, as a living organism, transcends the atoms, molecules and cells which make it up, so a community (or any social organisation in a culture) transcends the individual human beings who make it up. The forces that affect an individual human being (in a community) are not the same forces that affect the development of a community. To develop a leadership community, we must be able to see how a community transcends its members.

Dimensions of community

When we say a community is not the same thing as a human being, we say it does not have emotions, a head, thoughts, legs or a hobby. It does, however, have different parts to it, which apply to social organisations and culture rather than to individual human beings. One way to analyse a community is to use the six cultural "dimensions". These dimensions are (see figure 3.2):

- technological
- economic
- political
- institutional (social)
- aesthetic-value
- belief-conceptual

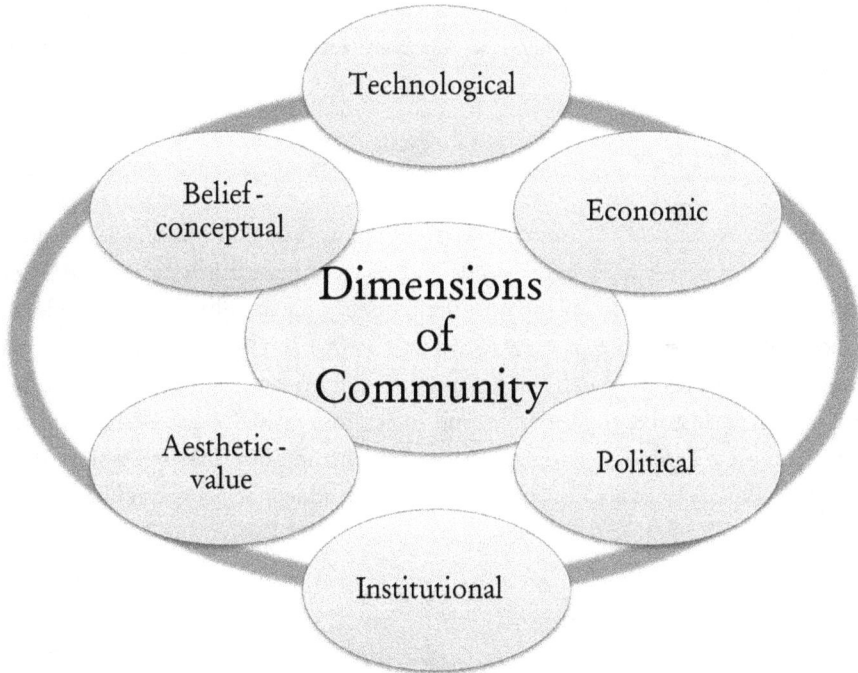

Figure 3.2 Dimensions of community

Each of these dimensions of community is transmitted by symbols and consists of systems of learned ideas and behaviour.

Technological dimension

The technological dimension of community is its capital, its tools and skills, and ways of dealing with the physical environment. It is not the physical tools themselves which make up the technological dimension of culture; it is the learned ideas and behaviour which allow humans to invent, use and teach others about tools. Technology is as much a cultural dimension as beliefs and patterns of interaction: it is symbolic. Technology is cultural. This cultural dimension is what the economist may call "real capital" (in contrast to financial capital). It is something valuable that is not produced for direct consumption, but to be used to increase production (therefore more wealth) in the future: investment.

In an organisation, technology includes desks, computers, paper, chairs, pens, office space, telephones, washrooms and lunch rooms. Some organisations have specific technology: footballs and uniforms for football clubs, blackboards, desks and chalk for schools, altars and pews for churches, transmitters and microphones for radio stations.

Through human history, technology has changed generally by becoming more complex and sophisticated and by gaining greater control over energy. One form does not immediately replace another. Usually changes are cumulative, with older tools and technologies dying out if they become relatively less useful, less efficient and more expensive.

Economic dimension

The economic dimension of community is its various ways and means of production and allocation of scarce and useful goods and services (wealth). It is not the physical items like cash which make up the economic dimension of culture, but the ideas and behaviour which give value to cash (and other items) for humans who have created the economic systems they use. As discussed in the previous section, over the broad course of human history, the general trend in economic change has been from simple to more complex. From an economic dimension this implies that one system did not immediately replace another, but new systems were added, and less useful ones slowly died out.

Political dimension

The political dimension of community is its various ways and means of allocating power, influence and decision-making. It is not the same as ideology, which belongs to the values dimension. It includes, but is not limited to, types of governance and management systems. It also includes how people in small or informal groups make decisions when they do not have a recognised leader. In the broad sweep of human history, leadership (power and influence) was at first diffuse, temporary and minimal. As history progressed, political systems become more complex, and power and influence increased and affected larger numbers of people. Communities, including the ones where you work, all have some political system, and there is some distance between the highest and lowest levels of power of individuals and groups.

Institutional dimension

The social or institutional dimension of community is composed of the ways people act, interact and react, and expect one another to act and interact. This dimension has to do with people's expectations, assumptions, judgements, predictions, responses and reactions. It looks at the patterns of relationships, sometimes identified as roles and status, and the formation of groups that derive from those patterns. The social organisation of the community is the sum total of all those interrelationships and patterns. The more effectively organised it is, the more capacity it has to achieve its organisational objectives or purpose.

As with the other dimensions, over the course of history the general movement has been from simple to complex. In early simple societies, the family was the community and the society. The family defined all roles and status. As societies became more complex, first the families became more complex, then new nonfamilial relationships developed and were recognised. Later the family itself declined in relative importance among all the many other kinds of relationship. Every time a new role is created, with its duties, responsibilities, rights and expected behaviour patterns, then the community becomes more complex.

Aesthetic values dimension

The aesthetic value dimension of community is the structure of ideas, sometimes paradoxical, inconsistent or contradictory, that people have about good and bad, beautiful and ugly and right and wrong, which are the justifications that people cite to explain their actions. The three axes along which people make judgements are all dependent upon what they learn from childhood and are all based upon social and community values.

Values are incredibly difficult to change in a community, especially if members perceive that an attempt is being made to change them. They do change, as community standards evolve, but that change cannot be rushed by outside influences or conscious manipulation. Shared community standards are important in community and personal identity; "who one is" is very much a matter of what values one believes in. The degree to which community or organisational members share values, and/or respect each other's values, is an important component of community.

Values tend to change as the community grows more complex, more heterogeneous, more connected to the world. It appears that there is no overall direction of change in human history: judgements become more liberal, more tolerant, more eclectic – or less – as societies become more complex and sophisticated. Communities at either end of the social complexity spectrum display standards of various degrees of rigidity. In spite of that range, within any community there is usually a narrow range of values.

Beliefs–conceptual dimension

The belief–conceptual dimension of community is another structure of ideas, also sometimes contradictory, that people have about the nature of the universe, the world around them, their role in it, cause and effect, and the nature of time, matter and behaviour. It includes shared beliefs about how this universe came to be, how it operates, and what is reality. When you drop a pencil onto the floor, you demonstrate your belief in gravity. When you say the sun comes up in the morning (of course it does not; the earth turns) you express your world view.

All six dimensions are in each bit of culture

The important thing to remember is that in any society, in any community, in any institution, in any interaction between individuals, there is an element of culture, and that includes something of each of these six cultural dimensions. The tools we use, the interactions we are engaged in, the beliefs and values we hold, are all part of our culture and part of our existence as social beings.

An important consideration in all this is the variety of interconnections between the cultural dimensions. They may be causally and functionally inter-related. Technology (in contrast to popularly held ideas), for example, both the tools and the skills to use them, is as much a part of culture or social system as are beliefs and ways of allocating wealth. Changes in any one dimension have repercussions in each of the other dimensions. Learning any new ways of doing things will require the learning of both new values and new perceptions. Changes in any dimension will start changes, like the ripples of water on a calm lake when you throw a stone into it, and ultimately all six dimensions will change. To change something in one cultural dimension not only **requires** changes in other dimensions, it **causes** changes in other dimensions.

Summary

In this section of the chapter, we took a slightly more academic route to describing what we mean by the word "community". Some of the key points from this section are:

- Community extends beyond its members.
- It has fuzzy boundaries.
- It can have subsections, but is also more than the sum of its parts.
- It can shift over time.
- It is not homogeneous.

- It is a cultural construct, and culture is learnt.

- It consists of a number of interrelated and interdependent dimensions.

With this little bit of theory under our belts, let us explore what leadership community may mean.

Defining a leadership community

One of the things we found really interesting in the process of thinking and writing about leadership community is that there appears to be very little formal writing on the subject. Even a Google search on the term produces a number of references to community leadership, issues related to community health and so forth. It would seem we are, at least for now, in unchartered waters!

In our own view, a corporate (or organisational) leadership community is:

- the leaders at all levels of the organisation

- who consciously share a common purpose and

- have a high degree of congruence, not only on the **how** of achieving the purpose, but also and more importantly the **why**.

This provisional and broad definition leads to a number of interesting questions, such as:

Can leadership exist only at the "top" of the organisation?	We do not believe so, and for a number of reasons such as:
	• The rate and complexity of change makes it impossible for the few at the "top" to ensure the re-novation[127] required to ensure long-term sustainability;
	• Broader society has shifted towards a value set of broader inclusivity.
Must purpose be "conscious"?	We think so. Although over time a leadership community may develop an intuitive awareness or sense of purpose, it is still useful (if not imperative) to constantly talk about and review purpose to prevent stagnation (and also to bring new members of the leadership community on board).
Can you be a leader in an organisation and not be part of the leadership community of that organisation?	Absolutely! This could happen 1) because the leadership community has not deliberately taken steps to make you part of the community, or 2) you have chosen not to be part of the leadership community.
Can a person move out of the leadership community?	Again, absolutely yes. People change over time, and it is entirely possible that the "fit" of the individual and the leadership community becomes misaligned.

| How do you know you have a vibrant and healthy leadership community? | At an emotional level, things will "feel" right. At a pragmatic level, no individual leader is irreplaceable. People will also be as comfortable to follow as they are to lead. |

Clearly, the key points from the preceding section (see Summary on page 42) also have some important potential implications for leadership community. Some of these are summarised in table 3.2.

Table 3.2 Leadership community implications

Key points	Implications
Community extends beyond its members.	In a global society as connected as ours is, formally and informally, there are people we are not necessarily even aware of that may exercise "leadership" over our organisation and its members.
It has fuzzy boundaries.	We have long been interested in the notion of co-opetition, or how companies can simultaneously compete and collaborate with other companies. Boundaries are neither static nor purely "logical". How leadership community plays out is therefore also not fully predictable.
It can have subsections, but is also more than the sum of its parts.	Leadership in organisations, almost by definition, follows an inside-out pattern. It starts with the individual, and then extends to the immediate team he or she is a member of, which forms part of the larger organisation, which of course is a subset of society at large. The challenge we have as leadership communities (and the members of these) is that all of these levels of engagement happen in real time and at the same time!
It can shift over time.	People change. Teams change. Companies change. Societies change. We would be foolish indeed to think that leadership community will not also change. The question therefore is not whether it changes, but whether we are able to at least in some mindful and deliberate manner steer or influence the direction of change.
It is not homogeneous.	Leadership community cannot be one monolithic thing. This is not philosophically desirable, nor practically do-able. The simple fact is that our leadership community will have a significant degree of diversity. What we have to figure out is what the "nonnegotiables" are that make us an identifiably different and valuable community.

Key points	Implications
It is a cultural construct, and culture is learnt.	Thank goodness we can teach culture, specifically organisational culture (or the dynamics of our leadership community). If we could not, it would definitely have a very limited lifespan! Of course, the fact that we can teach it does not mean that every person will want to learn it, and how we choose to deal with this is also part of the character of our leadership community.
It consists of a number of interrelated and interdependent dimensions.	It is indeed a cliché that "everything is connected to everything else". One of the challenges for leadership communities is that this also means the inherent complexity of what we deal with is increasing, which places ever-growing demands on the ability of the members of our leadership community to generate the requisite complexity and demonstrate the value sets appropriate to such complexity.

An important (and perhaps less obvious) implication of this description of leadership community, is that much of its existence depends not only on the decisions taken at an organisational level, but also at the level of the individual. At a personal level, the challenge becomes one of making sure that we are part of a leadership community that creates the context within which we can become the best that we can possibly be.

At the heart of the matter lies the simple aspiration that the organisation has to build and entrench leadership excellence in a mindful and deliberate manner. So how does a company build leadership excellence into its leadership community?

Creating and maintaining leadership community excellence

Building leadership community excellence is conceptually not too difficult to do. In practice though, it is a journey of fundamental transformation, not only at an organisational level but also (and perhaps in the first instance!) at a deeply personal level.

Figure 3.3 is a reflection of the typical "steps" we work through with clients wishing to embark on building leadership excellence as part of an overall business strategy. This approach is very similar to that reported on by the Taleo Corporation[128] and the Center for Creative Leadership.[129]

Figure 3.3 Building leadership excellence

In the following paragraphs, we explore each of the steps in a little more detail.

Business context and strategy

This step is not about having strategic planning workshops, but having one or more conversations about the organisation's business environment, history and vision so that building leadership excellence can be clearly and specifically positioned as part of overall strategic business intent.[130] We advise clients that unless they can specifically articulate the business benefits to be derived from leadership interventions, 1) they will not be in a position to measure impact or benefit, and therefore 2) any intervention will do (they will just not be sure what!).

Define the leadership stance

This step is about defining the specifics of what the organisation means by the word "leadership". Every person in your organisation has his or her own favourite leadership theory, so do not assume you are talking about the same thing when you talk about leadership. Just some of the questions that should be addressed are:

- Is "leadership" just the executives and managers, or does leadership exist at all levels of the organisation?

- What is our definition of leadership – is it about leadership style, leadership roles or something else?

- What should we do about aspects such as diversity, succession management, recruitment, selection and development?

Document the leadership strategy

As with any other business strategy, it makes good sense to document your leadership excellence strategy. The issue is of course not the document per se, but the process the organisation goes through to end up with such a document. And let us be clear about this, we are not talking about a "bosberaad" type of approach where the senior executives, with the help of a consultant, dream up a leadership strategy and then announce it to the rest of the organisation. For one of our clients, this process was a hugely collaborative one where leaders at different levels had the opportunity to contribute to the leadership strategy document. Of course this takes time, but the benefit of having the conversations which lead to early shared understanding and alignment is in and of itself part of building leadership excellence.

As the organisation moves through the next steps, it will also find that documenting the leadership strategy is an iterative and evolving process.

Leadership talent systems

With a documented leadership strategy, the next phase is to ensure that the systems to execute the strategy are in place. At a practical level, this means that at the very least the governance structures and the specific leadership behaviours (competence framework) need to be defined. Some of this work is very technical in nature, so that some expertise in terms of, for example, levels of work and leadership theory and practice is required. Having said this, a collaborative approach to defining these is still advisable.

A key aspect at this stage is defining required leadership behaviours in such a manner that they support the leadership stance the organisation wishes to adopt. Although there are frameworks available (such as Lominger®, DDI®, Hall® and others) we usually advise organisations to see these as a point of departure in building a framework that is unique and specific to their own leadership stance and leadership strategy.

Leadership talent identification

With a clear articulation of the required leadership behaviours, it becomes a fairly simple (if slightly technical) process to identify the most appropriate talent identification (assessment) processes. In our view, even more important than selecting the right assessment "tools" is being very clear and specific about the way in which these will be introduced and used in the organisation. Regardless of the tools chosen, the process itself can cause great anxiety and even harm, so that careful thought about the **purpose** and **process** of leadership talent assessment is required. (See chapter 6 for more detail).

Leadership talent development

Most organisations think about leadership development purely from a formal perspective, in other words the programmes leaders are sent on. Research however shows that formal development accounts for only 10 to 20 per cent of leadership development, while the rest is through informal development processes such as experiential learning, coaching and other interventions. It is also important to acknowledge that in this context "informal" does not mean "unplanned". In fact, the work we do with our clients means that all the formal and informal leadership development processes are carefully planned in great detail so that they form an integrated whole.

This approach means that leadership development processes become part and parcel of the organisation's talent management strategy through career and succession planning and management. (See chapter 8 for more detail).

Leadership excellence review

This is the step in the building of leadership capacity and excellence where we link all the preceding work with business context and strategy. The question, to remind the reader, is not a simple ROI one, but rather a benefits realisation one. In our view, some of the questions that should be asked are:

- Do participants in the leadership assessment and development processes give positive feedback on their experiences?
- Do we see a change in the day-to-day behaviour of our leadership?
- Do we see an improvement in the performance levels of leaders at all levels?
- Do our employees display more engaged (committed) behaviour?
- What do our client satisfaction surveys indicate?
- Are there improvements in efficiencies, costs, sales?

- Are we increasingly able to recruit and promote from within?

- What do other companies think of us and our people?

- Are we finding it easier to attract the "right" people from outside?

Of course, it will be difficult to demonstrate a direct linear relationship between leadership excellence and all of these issues. After all, the organisation is a complex social system with many interdependencies. At some point, the executive team should ask itself simply: "Do we want to stop the leadership capacity-building process, or is it working for us?"

What does it do for your business?

This section introduces at a very basic level the idea of the business benefit of leadership community excellence. Chapter 8 goes into significantly more detail on the philosophical and practical aspects of the measurement of business benefits realisation associated with leadership excellence.

The business logic

As is shown in figure 3.4, leadership excellence is a key driver in articulating business strategy. Clearly, if you have an organisation with weak and ineffectual leadership you are unlikely to be able to formulate and execute a business strategy that will deliver sustainable competitive advantage. Such a business strategy should clearly focus on both the external environment (competitive landscape, opportunities and threats) and the internal capacity to execute business strategy.

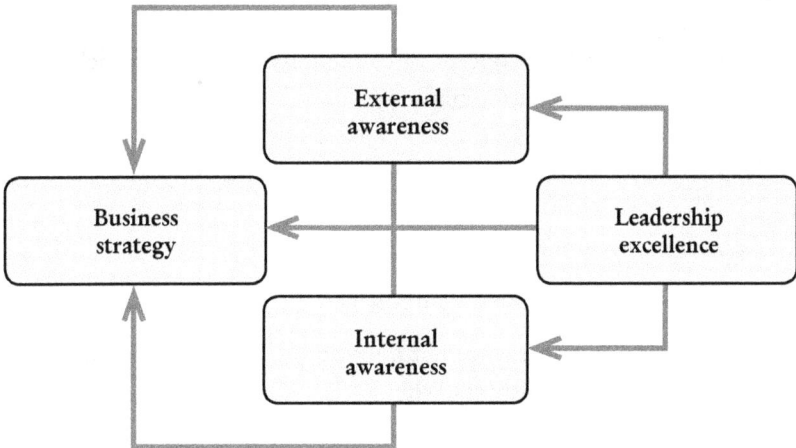

Figure 3.4 Business logic Step 1

As shown in figure 3.5, leadership excellence is in and of itself not sufficient to drive business results. Having leadership excellence is, however, a key driver of employee engagement (or organisation culture or internal leadership brand) which in turn is a key driver of the customer (or stakeholder) experience (or external brand). It is the customer experience that finally drives business results (of course, not purely on its own).

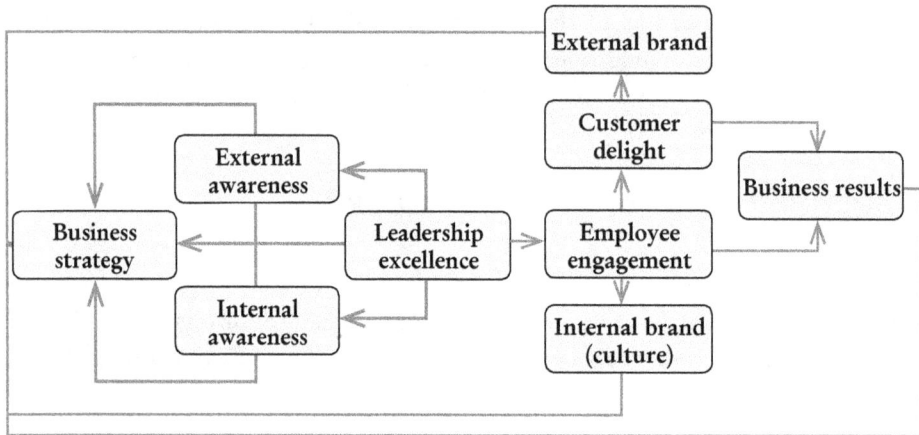

Figure 3.5 Business logic Step 2

In simple terms, we are therefore suggesting that leadership community excellence will lead to the type of internal culture where employee engagement and commitment drive customer (or stakeholder) delight, which simultaneously drives a positive external brand and sustainable business results (measured along more dimensions than simply growth or financial results).

Closing remarks

In this chapter we explored the concept of community. We then unpacked what was meant by the corporate leadership community.

In our view, a corporate (or organisational) leadership community is:

- the leaders at all levels of the organisation

- who consciously share a common purpose and

- have a high degree of congruence not only on the **how** of achieving the purpose, but also and more importantly the **why**.

In the next chapter we explore the people who form the leadership community.

Chapter 4

Leaders are people too

Letitia van der Merwe

❄

"Every man of action has a strong dose of egotism, pride, hardness, and cunning. But all those things will be forgiven him, indeed, they will be regarded as high qualities, if he can make them the means to achieve great ends."
– Charles De Gaulle

"What the persona does is what the world sees, but something very different may be happening deep inside, where our private self hides."
– Manfred Kets de Vries

Chapter 2 explored the changing leadership landscape so as to create a thinking framework for the rest of the book. The new leadership landscape was unpacked and we highlighted some implications for leadership in organisations. As also mentioned in chapter 2, for decades literature and research on business leadership have been characterised by a search for "good" or "effective" leadership. This search for the Holy Grail of leadership has led to business leadership being romanticised (the "hero") or in some cases even seen in terms of religion (the "saviour"). Just consider the quotes below:

- Good leadership consists of showing average people how to do the work of superior people. – John D Rockefeller

- A leader is one who knows the way, goes the way, and shows the way. – John C Maxwell

- Leadership is lifting a person's vision to high sights, the raising of a person's performance to a higher standard, the building of a personality beyond its normal limitations. – Peter Drucker

- Leadership is the art of getting someone else to do something you want done because he wants to do it. – General Dwight Eisenhower

The consequence of this is that business leaders (and, in many instances, leaders) are required to act as the heroes or saviours of organisations. This also reinforces the notion that leadership knows best, even to the extent that leadership has almost became sacred. However, we know that in reality not all leadership is conducive to the good of the organisation.

In order to lead an effective organisation one needs to understand the dynamics of leadership. As mentioned in chapter 3, the whole notion of leadership community is that leadership is never limited to the "heroic" acts of one individual leader; rather it operates in the context of people, the business, the industry and the larger social environment.

We expect a lot from our leaders – both in terms of their work and their nature. To cope with these pressures, leaders have developed a facade of being in control – they feel they need to live up to idealised images of being successful. However, if leaders over-identify with these images of success, they may give rise to a number of psychological pressures and cause leaders to damage organisations.

Consequently, a rise in psychological pressures on leadership, particularly at executive level, has been identified by Kets de Vries et al.[131] Key factors contributing to these pressures are: loneliness, being watched by others, concerns about high performance expectations in one's role, a steep learning curve given the turbulent environment, time constraints and work–life balance.

In the previous chapters we commented that we are starting to see a movement from more individual approaches (ie leadership as a position) to those that are more collective (ie leadership as a process). We believe organisations will continue to move toward viewing leadership as a collective process that happens throughout the organisation through interdependent decision-making.

Coming from the behavioural sciences, what intrigues me about leadership is the behaviour of the collective and where this stems from. What we are arguing is that we cannot even start to contemplate leadership talent assessment and development until we actually have some understanding of the nature or being of leaders.

The nature of leadership

In this chapter we explore the human nature of leadership. In this section we explore different themes, namely the cognitive and emotional nature of leaders.

How do you view the nature of leadership?		
Study the following statements and label them true or false.	True	False
• Good leaders are rational objective decision-makers. • Good leaders will always do what is right. • Leaders are supposed to always know the way and save the organisation from disasters. • The "soft" side of leadership is of no consequence. Systems and process will always prevail. • Leadership personality has no effect on the behaviour of followers.		

These questions offer a preview of the themes that will be discussed. If you've labelled all of them "true", we have some convincing to do.

Irrational rationality

First we discuss the issue of irrational leadership behaviour inside organisations. Classical economics held that people are rational, self-interested and have a firm grasp on self-control. Behavioural economics (and common sense) showed instead that we are not as logical as we might think, we do care about others, and we are not as disciplined as we would like to be. For example, one of the most infamous financial events in recent memory is the bursting of the internet bubble. How could something so catastrophic be allowed to happen over and over again?

A few years ago I engaged with an executive leader in an organisation after a spectacular business failure. For some reason the executive leadership team had opted for a business strategy that didn't make sense and placed an enormous burden on the organisation in terms of cash flow. When I asked the executive leader for the rationale behind the decisions, he just couldn't answer me.

Maybe one answer lies in the concept of "irrational rationality". The concept was popularised by the economist Bryan Caplan in 2001. The theory is that, when the costs of having erroneous beliefs are low, people relax their intellectual standards and allow themselves to be more easily influenced by fallacious reasoning, cognitive biases and emotional appeals. In other words, people do not deliberately seek to believe false things, but rather stop putting in the intellectual effort to be open to evidence that may contradict their beliefs.

Cognitive biases

Cognitive biases are tendencies to think in certain ways. Cognitive biases can lead to systematic deviations from a standard of rationality or good judgment. Below are a number of these biases (unfortunately the author is unknown).

Anchoring: The tendency for first impressions, even irrelevant ones, to continue to influence decision-making. Students were asked to estimate the number of nations in Africa. Before they estimated it, a wheel with the numbers 1–100 on it was spun to generate a random number. Those for whom the wheel came up 12 consistently estimated lower than those for whom the wheel came up 92, even though there is obviously no relation between the random number from the wheel and the actual number of African nations.

Availability bias: Our tendency to base evaluations of probability on the ease with which examples are recalled. However, ease of recall can be for reasons that have nothing to do with actual frequency. Shark attacks and aeroplane crashes are easy to recall because of their emotional salience; as a result we tend to greatly overestimate their frequency. A special case of this is the so-called "flashbulb memory", a memory of where we were or what we were doing when some especially noteworthy or emotionally charged happened. Experimental studies reveal that these flashbulb memories, about which we are supremely confident, are in fact no more likely to be true than other memories.

Barnum effect: Named for famed circus administrator PT Barnum, this is our tendency to believe that descriptions of us are accurate as long as we think that those descriptions were intended to be about us. More generally, it involves interpreting ambiguous data in ways that make it seem accurate. For example, people given the same personality description all rate it as an accurate description of themselves when led to believe that it was generated specifically for them.

Base rate neglect: When making judgments about probabilities, we often ignore base rates in favour of good stories. Base rate data tells us how representative one feature is of a whole population, or how likely an event is to occur independently of specific conditions. For example, from the fact that most men who have committed sexual assault have used pornography, we often conclude that pornography causes sexual assault. The missing base rate data is what percentage of men, independently of whether they have committed sexual assault, has used pornography.

Confirmation bias: Our tendency to seek out and more effectively recall evidence that confirms a hypothesis rather than evidence that disconfirms it. It also refers to our tendency to interpret ambiguous evidence in a way that supports rather than refutes the hypothesis in question. Related to this is our tendency to evaluate evidence supportive of our beliefs less critically than evidence that potentially refutes our beliefs, and to be more likely to remember the confirmatory evidence.

Conjunction effect: When given two statements, A and B, we often judge A and B together to be more likely than A or B alone. This is generally true when A and B seem to "fit" well. For example, we tend to judge that the claim "Jennifer is a feminist philosopher" is more likely than either "Jennifer is a feminist" or "Jennifer is a philosopher" because being a philosopher seems to "fit" with being a feminist. In reality, the likelihood of any two claims both being true is less than the likelihood that either alone is true.

False consensus effect: Our tendency to overestimate the degree to which others are similar to us in their beliefs, experiences, values or characteristics.

In-group favouritism: Our tendency to empathise with (and hence consider the interests of) others based on the degree to which they are similar to us, and hence familiar. This is independent of considerations of bias in the judgemental sense.

Lake Wobegon effect: Named after the fictional town where "every child is above average", this names our tendency to overrate our abilities compared to others. For example, most people rate themselves as above average in intelligence, leadership ability, studiousness, job performance and driving ability; almost no one rates themselves as below average in these things.

Overclaiming: Our tendency to overestimate the value and impact of our own contribution, due to our greater awareness of it. This can often lead us to self-serving and profoundly unjust accounts of what is fair and/or deserved.

What I am trying to illustrate is that leaders are not the rational people we would expect. Albert Ellis, a pioneer in rational emotive therapy, discusses how behaviours are a result of cognitions (beliefs) about an event or situation and that the cognitions can be classified as rational or irrational. The resulting behaviours (barring the presence of psychosis) will be logical, although they may be either rational or irrational.

Problems start to occur for leaders when they assume they understand what the beliefs of employees are (often assuming that these beliefs are the same as the leader's) and are surprised when an employee responds in what they consider to be an illogical and irrational way; however, the response is really coming from the employee's different frame of reference. Secondly, leadership irrationality is prevalent and can cause 1) new ways of solving problems or 2) havoc in organisations.

Personality

The traditional approach to leadership and personality suggested that people are born with special traits that make them great leaders. Robbins[132] claims that there are at least four limitations to the personality theory or trait theory:

- There are no universal traits that predict leadership in all situations. There are, however, traits that predict leadership in selective situations.

- Traits predict behaviour more often in weak situations than in strong situations. The strong situations are those in which strong behavioural norms exist, including strong incentives for specific behaviours and clearly defined expectations of which behaviours are rewarded and which punished. These strong situations in turn create less opportunity for leaders to express their inherent dispositional tendencies. In many organisations, a highly structured, formal culture exists, which fits the description of a strong situation, therefore limiting the power of traits to predict leadership.

- There is no clear evidence of differentiating between cause and effect. In other words, are leaders self-confident or does becoming successful build the leader's self-confidence?

- Traits do not distinguish between effective and ineffective leaders; rather, they seem to be more accurate at predicting the appearance of leadership.

A meta-study in 2002[133] indicated that the personalities of managers directly impact the level of employee engagement or satisfaction, making it worthwhile for leaders to understand their personalities and the impact of their behaviours on others. Within this theme of leadership personality there are two key aspects for us to understand: 1) how it impacts leadership success in the workplace and 2) how it impacts leadership failure in the workplace.

How the nature of leadership manifests in the workplace

In the previous section we looked at the nature of leadership. In our quest to understand leaders as human beings, this section explores three key themes in terms of how the nature of leadership unfolds in the workplace:

- emotional intelligence
- leadership identity
- the darker side of leadership

This is not about "soft" issues, but about the real "stuff". It is about leaders, all of us, taking personal responsibility and accountability for both our being and our behaviour. Each one of us will leave some legacy, and each one of us has a choice as to what this legacy will be.

Emotional Intelligence (EQ)

Linking to the rationality argument is the notion of emotional intelligence. Yes, we also expect our leaders to behave with emotional intelligence. We expect them to care about us as individuals, treat us with respect, understand our problems and display empathy, and never to treat us unfairly or emotionally inconsiderately.

Daniel Goleman introduced the concept of EQ in 1995 in his bestseller *Emotional Intelligence*. Goleman's belief is that emotional competencies are twice as important to people's success today as raw intelligence or technical know-how. He also argues that the further up the corporate ranks you go, the more important emotional intelligence becomes. EQ consists of four key components, as depicted in table 4.1.

Table 4.1: Components of Emotional Intelligence[134]

	SELF (Intrapersonal = how we manage ourselves)	**SOCIAL** (Interpersonal = how we manage our relationships)
RECOGNITION	**SELF-AWARENESS** **Emotional self-awareness** (Reading one's own emotions & recognising their impact; using "gut sense" to guide decisions) **Accurate self-assessment** (Knowing one's strengths & limits) **Self-confidence** (A sound sense of one's self-worth & capabilities)	**SOCIAL AWARENESS** **Empathy** (Sensing others' emotions, understanding their perspective & taking an interest in their concerns) **Organisational awareness** (Reading the currents, decision networks & politics at organisational level) **Service orientation** (Recognising & meeting follower, client or customer needs)
REGULATION	**SELF-MANAGEMENT** **Self-control** (Keeping disruptive emotions & impulses under control) **Transparency** (Displaying honesty & integrity; trustworthiness) **Adaptability** (Flexibility in adapting to changing situations or overcoming obstacles) **Achievement drive** (The drive to improve performance to meet inner standards of excellence) **Initiative** (Readiness to act & seize opportunities) **Optimism** (Seeing the upside in events)	**RELATIONSHIP MANAGEMENT** **Inspiring leadership** (Guiding and motivating with a compelling vision) **Developing others** (Bolstering others' abilities through feedback & guidance) **Influence** (Wielding a range of tactics for persuasion) **Change catalyst** (Initiating, managing & leading in a new direction) **Conflict management** (Resolving disagreements) **Building Bonds** (Cultivating & maintaining a web of relationships) **Teamwork and collaboration** (Cooperation & team building)

Source: Goleman's Emotional Intelligence Model (2002)

Emotional contagion

One process through which people influence each other (un)consciously in organisations is emotional contagion. It is described as the tendency to automatically mimic and synchronise facial expressions, vocalisations, postures and movements with those of another person and, consequently, to converge emotionally. More important than knowing exactly how emotional contagion works is being aware that it exists and understanding its influence on organisational life.

Goleman, Boyatzis and McKee[135] elaborate five competencies in which the effective use of the emotions of other people (or the principle of emotional contagion) is essential:

- *Influencing.* The effective use of influencing tactics is based on inducing certain feelings in other people – for instance, enthusiasm for a project or the passion to outdo a competitor.

- *Communication.* Sending clear and convincing messages starts with the ability to know what others feel about something and how they will react, and adapting your message accordingly.

- *Conflict management.* Negotiating and solving conflicts is to a large extent a process of emotional influencing rather than a purely rational process.

- *Leadership.* Inspiring and coaching employees is based on the effective communication of feelings in a two-way direction.

- *Change movement.* The effective communication and implementation of change processes require a high level of emotional appeal and influence to break down people's resistance.

Emotional labour

Related to the study of emotional contagion is the recently developed research field dealing with how people manage their emotions in the workplace, known as **emotional labour**. Arlie Hochschild[136] created the term "emotional labour" in 1983 to describe the things that service workers do that go beyond physical or mental duties.

Given that people experience a wide range of emotions during any given workday, emotions that are felt and those that are required may not always be congruent with each other. When such a mismatch occurs, an employee may choose to ignore the prescribed display rules and express genuine emotions during stressful encounters. Such emotional deviance may be detrimental to one's wellbeing, however, especially if the employee identifies with the occupation and its display rules (eg a counsellor's curt response to a client). On other occasions, there may be a discrepancy between expressed and felt emotions, creating the experience of emotional dissonance, which has been associated with a range of negative psychological outcomes.[137]

Leader identity

In its simplest form leader identity refers to "the question of who I am and who I am striving to become." In my observation it seems that leaders experience tensions in seeking a stable sense of identity in the face of the contradictory forces and insecurities inherent in identity construction, which seems to be predominantly influenced by social relations within the workplace.

These observations are supported by research conducted by Komives, Mainella, Longerbeam, Osteen and Owenstating[138] in 2006. They found that the five categories that influenced the development of a leadership identity were: broadening view of leadership; developing self; group influences; developmental influences; and the changing view of self with others. This Leader Identity Development model (LID) is shown in table 4.2.

The LID model is stage-based and entails leaders progressing through one stage before beginning the next (see table 4.2). Researchers have long recognised that the term "stages" is more complex than a linear representation might imply. Stages are linear, but they are also cyclical. Even as development through the stages occurs, development proceeds in a circular manner. A helix model of development allows for stages to be repeatedly experienced, and each return is experienced with a deeper and more complex understanding and performing of the stage. Development is not only cyclical, but also complex. The achievement of each stage is influenced by a myriad of contextual factors in the environment and by each individual's different stage of readiness.

As can be seen from the literature, leadership identity development is an iterative and dynamic process occurring through the interaction between giving recognition and being recognised or affirmed. As a result, if leadership is experienced and affirmed positively it will build a positive leader identity, encouraging the leader to seek further development opportunities.

If we take into account the impact of the demands that the workplace and stakeholders place on leaders, the preferred leader identity may not be realised, leading to a form of identity marked by self-doubt and extreme self-consciousness. This links to the next section where we explore the darker side of leadership.

Table 4.2: Leadership identity development model

Stages →	**1** Awareness		**2** Exploration/engagement		**3** Leader identified	
Key categories		*Transition*		*Transition*	*Emerging*	*Immersion*
Stage descriptions	* recognising that leadership is happening around you * getting exposure to involvements	"I am not a leader."	*intentional involvements (sports, religious institutions, service, scouts, dance, SGA) *experiencing groups for the first time *taking on responsibilities		*trying on new roles *identifying skills needed *taking on individual responsibility *individual accomplishments important	*getting things done *managing others *practising different approaches/styles *leadership seen largely as positional roles held by self or others; leaders do leadership
Broadening view of leadership	* other people are leaders; leaders are out there somewhere	"I am not a leader."	"I want to be involved."	"I want to do more."	"A leader gets things done."	"I am the leader and others follow me" or "I am a follower looking to the leaders for direction."
Developing self	*becoming aware of national leaders and authority figures (eg the principal)	*wanting to make friends	*develop personal skills *identify personal strengths/ weaknesses *prepare for leadership *build self-confidence	*recognise personal leadership potential *motivation to change something	*positional leadership roles or group member roles *narrow down to meaningful experiences (eg sports, clubs, yearbook, scouts, class projects)	*models others *leader struggles with delegation *moves in and out of leadership roles and member roles but still believes the leader is in charge *appreciates individual recognition

Stages →	1 Awareness		2 Exploration/engagement		3 Leader identified	
Key categories		Transition		Transition	Emerging	Immersion
Group influences	*uninvolved or "inactive" follower	*wanting to get involved	*"activate" follower or member *engage in diverse contexts (eg sports, clubs, class projects)	narrow interests	*leader has to get things done *group has a job to do; organise to get tasks done	*involve members to get the job done *stick with a primary group as an identity base; explore other groups
Developmental influences	affirmation by adults (parents, teachers, coaches, scout leaders, religious elders)	*observation/ watching *recognition *adult sponsors	*affirmation of adults *attributions (others see me as a leader)	*role models *older peers as sponsors *adult sponsors *assume positional roles *reflection/retreat	take on responsibilities	*model older peers and adults *observe older peers *adults as mentors, guides, coaches
Changing view of self with others	Dependent				Independent Dependent	

Table 4.2: Leadership identity development model (continued)

The key	4 Leadership differentiated				5 Generativity		6 Integration/synthesis
	Transition	*Emerging*	*Immersion*	*Transition*	*Generativity*	*Transition*	
*shifting order of consciousness *take on more complex leadership challenges		*joining with others in shared tasks/goals from positional or nonpositional group roles *need to learn group skills *new belief that leadership can come from anywhere in the group (nonpositional)	*seeks to facilitate a good group process whether in positional or nonpositional leader role *commitment to community of the group awareness that leadership is a group process		*active commitment to a personal passion *accepting responsibility for the development of others *promotes team learning *responsible for sustaining organisations		*continued self-development and life-long learning *striving for congruence and internal confidence
"Holding a position does not mean I am a leader."		"I need to lead in a participatory way and I can contribute to leadership from anywhere in the organisation"; "I can be a leader without a title"; "I am a leader even if I am not the leader."	"Leadership is happening everywhere; leadership is a process; we are doing leadership together; we are all responsible."	"Who's coming after me?"	"I am responsible as a member of my communities to facilitate the development of others as leaders and enrich the life of our groups."	"I need to be true to myself in all situations and open to growth."	"I know I am able to work effectively with others to accomplish change from any place in the organisation"; "I am a leader."

The key	4 Leadership differentiated				5 Generativity		6 Integration/synthesis
Transition	*Emerging*	*Immersion*	*Transition*		*Transition*	
*recognition that I cannot do it all myself *learn to value the importance/talent of others	*learn to trust and value others and their involvement *openness to other perspectives *develop comfort leading as an active member *let go of control	*learns about personal influence *effective in both positional and nonpositional roles *practises being engaged member *values servant leadership	*focus on passion, vision and commitments *wants to serve society	*sponsor and develop others *transforming leadership *concern for leadership pipeline *concerned with sustainability of ideas	*openness to ideas *learning from others	*sees leadership as a lifelong development process *wants to leave things better *"I am trustworthy and value that I have credibility" *recognition of role modelling to others
*meaningfully engage with others *look to group resources	*seeing the collective whole; the big picture *learning group and team skills	*value teams *value connectedness to others *learn how the system works	*value process *seek fit with organisation's vision	*sustain the organisation ensuring continuity in areas of passion/focus	*anticipating transition to new roles	*sees organisational complexity across contexts *can imagine how to engage with different organisations
*older peers as sponsors and mentors *adults as mentors and meaning-makers *learning about leadership	*practising leadership in ongoing peer relationships	*responds to meaning-makers (student affairs staff, key faculty, same-age peer mentors)	*begins coaching others	*responds to meaning-makers (student affairs staff, same-age peer mentors)	*shared learning *reflection/retreat	*recycles when context changes or is uncertain (contextual uncertainty) *enables continual recycling through leadership stages

Interdependent

The darker side of leadership

"Fear is the path to the dark side. Fear leads to anger. Anger leads to hate. Hate leads to suffering." Yoda – fictional character in the *Star Wars* movies

Perhaps George Lucas has succeeded in creating one of the greatest cautionary tales for the aspiring leader in his portrayal of Darth Vader's devastating reign of terror in the *Star Wars* movies. Darth Vader embodies behaviours that make most contemporary leadership scholars cringe.

The dark side of leadership is a duality, in which the very strengths that leaders treasure and are admired for can become their worst liabilities. Henry Adams, a journalist, historian and active observer of people, concluded in his autobiography:

> The effect of power and publicity on all men is the aggravation of self, a sort of tumour that ends by killing the victim's sympathies; a diseased appetite, like a passion for drink or perverted tastes; one can scarcely use expressions too strong to describe the violence of egotism it stimulates.[139]

Literature on the leadership dark side doesn't seem to provide a unified definition. The focus of literature in this field is more on the particular characteristics of toxic behaviour, for example "people are rewarded for agreeing with the leader and punished for thinking differently"[140] and personality traits of the leader, for example narcissism and lack of self-esteem.[141]

Slattery[142] refers to the dark side of leadership and proposes a useful definition also applicable to toxic leadership: "an on-going pattern of behaviour exhibited by a leader that results in overall negative organisational outcomes based on the interactions between the leader, follower and the environment. Organisational goals, morale and follower satisfaction are thwarted through the abuse of power and self-interest of the leader."

This definition is useful, as it considers:

1. **The leader him- or herself**. The abuse of power and self-interest of both leader and followers is implicitly described in the definition. Leaders have their own predispositions and psychological make-up that impact on their behaviour.

2. **The contribution of followers to the leadership process**. Leadership cannot exist without followership. Followers are integral to the performance of leadership. Followers can contribute to negative organisational outcomes by complying with unethical behaviours or actively undermining the leader. By this we are not suggesting the leader is the result of the followers, merely that the leader–follower relationship will have an impact on the leadership behaviour.[143]

3. **The environment**. Lastly, the environment consists of the situational variables that have been demonstrated to impact on leader behaviour; for example, the real (or assumed) requirements or organisational demands placed on leaders.

Traditionally leadership development was viewed as only assessing the gap between strengths and weaknesses and then putting plans in place to close this gap. My thinking was fundamentally challenged by the work of Hogan. According to Hogan, the very strengths that leaders treasure and are admired for can become liabilities under certain circumstances. In many cases the qualities of a leader have both a positive and a negative face. Hogan observes that many leadership behavioural problems can be ascribed to overusing strengths. For us this has become evident in 360° assessment surveys with leaders that we use to determine leadership competence. One can often link "not yet competent" scores in problem behaviour to "highly developed" scores in overused skills. When under pressure, most people will display certain counterproductive tendencies. Hogan[144] refers to these as possible leadership derailers. Under normal conditions these characteristics may actually be strengths.

However, when a person is tired, pressured, bored or otherwise distracted, these risk factors may impede that person's effectiveness and erode the quality of his or her relationship with customers, colleagues and those that report to him or her. Others may be aware of these tendencies, but may not give the person any feedback on them. For example, the ability to influence others is usually a key requirement for leadership within an organisation. But when does it become manipulation?

Case in point

Extract from an interview with Manfred Kets de Vries

... narcissism is a clinically recognised disorder. In an oversimplified way, it can be viewed as a pathological reaction to problems concerning self-worth. It manifests itself in the need to prove to yourself that you are special, and entitled to special treatment. Other indicators include a need for constant attention and admiration, selfishness, a lack of empathy, the exploitation of others, and enviousness.

Narcissistic people may evade rules and regulations; their attitude is that these apply only to others. They may throw tantrums when they don't get their way. Their outbursts of rage can be phenomenal. But some of their behaviour can be interpreted by others as quite charismatic. And thus they often rise to lead large organisations and put a strong stamp on them.

> **Case in point**
>
> Keep in mind that narcissism in itself isn't a bad thing; it's part of our makeup. It may have received a bad reputation because of the Greek myth of Narcissus, the youth who fell in love with his reflection. But in moderation, the condition is natural and even necessary. It contributes to assertiveness, self-confidence, and creativity. These are all very desirable qualities for business leaders. People who achieve things – who write books, who run companies, who oversee projects – have to be somewhat narcissistic, or they wouldn't be motivated to excellence. Some of our most gifted leaders have evident narcissism. John Harvey-Jones, for instance, the head of Imperial Chemical Industries [ICI] during the 1980s and host of a BBC television show called Trouble-shooter in the 1990s, was a charismatic individual, with wild eyes, wild ties, and wild hair. He was also a consummate, constructive narcissist.

Leadership community: the antidote to the leadership dark side

"There is no such thing as leadership by the masses." – Dowd (1936)

Leaders may exhibit the dark side of leadership because of a range of factors. There seems to be little empirical evidence pointing to definite causation. Research indicates that a leader may move from being "constructive" to "destructive" as a result of situational factors or personality traits.

Although some dark side behaviour causes serious problems, many business organisations tend to reinforce and exaggerate some of this behaviour. Consider for example the bold and domineering manager who is praised and rewarded for getting the job done. Or the charismatic leader who is famous for being able to empathise with those he or she leads. This enables them to pursue their own ends without restraint.

The first step in minimising the effect of dark side behaviour is to recognise that these behaviours exist. The next step is to recognise that the only way to reduce this dysfunctional behaviour is to address it through the leadership community – a leadership community that can outlast individual leaders.

> **Some of the things organisations may want to do:**
>
> - Have **real** conversations about the organisation's leadership brand.
> - Extend these conversations throughout the organisation.
> - Assess their current status (bench strength) in terms of the leadership community.
> - Give people the opportunity to discover for themselves who they are.
> - Plan carefully the processes of developing leadership capacity (rather than focusing on the content of courses).
> - Be rigorous in weeding out leaders who do not match the leadership brand.
> - Make sure that organisational systems, processes and culture are aligned to the leadership brand.

Admittedly there are different expectations for leaders. At the same time, leaders perpetuate the intensity of expectation by trying to live up to some mythical set of criteria of the "ideal leader", propagated by popular (and pseudo-academic!) literature. Be the best leader that you can be. Understand the image in the mirror and come to terms with it. Be authentic.

Summary

In this chapter we argued that a lot of our thinking about leadership is informed by our own mental models. We asked the reader to explore what the human side of leaders means and how it impacts on both good and bad leadership. The chapter concluded by arguing that building leadership community is the antidote to bad leadership – that the community can prevent an organisation from going toxic and displaying toxic leadership behaviour.

In the next chapter we explore the concept of leadership (the soul of the community) and how to build these brand enabling conditions, especially from the perspective of the Human Resources Leader.

Chapter 5

Creating leadership brand enabling conditions

Anton Verwey

Contributing author: Charles du Toit

❄

"In this ever-changing society, the most powerful and enduring brands are built from the heart. They are real and sustainable. Their foundations are stronger because they are built with the strength of the human spirit, not an ad campaign. The companies that are lasting are those that are authentic." **– Howard Schultz**

"A brand for a company is like a reputation for a person. You earn reputation by trying to do hard things well." **– Jeff Bezos**

In this chapter we explore the role that the HR professional should play in creating a set of organisational conditions in which leadership excellence is created and developed. Clearly, this role takes place within the context of a different perspective on the leadership landscape, as well as our thinking frameworks on leadership community and the identification and development of "the leader" and the "leadership community".

In a recent debate in the HR Executive Forum on LinkedIn, a question was posed: "does HR deserve a seat at the [boardroom] table?" This debate, unlike most, raged across the world, with hundreds of posts with varying points of view ranging from "no" to the most popular, "yes, as a business partner." HR is a business partner with a deep knowledge of the business, ensuring that the business is staffed by capable people. This widely accepted HR role was first popularised by Ulrich some 20 years ago. The recognition of this role has to some degree shifted HR practitioners from the "personnel manager" image and it has certainly brought into focus the critical need for HR practitioners who truly understand the business aspects of their employer, if they are going to contribute meaningfully.

However, this role of business partner is not unique to the field of HR. Surely IT services need to have similar business savvy in order to support business's needs in their field of expertise, and the same is required of marketing services and, depending on the industry, technical and engineering and even production services.

It has also become increasingly accepted that the primary leadership relationship between employer and subordinate exists between the line leader and employee, and that at best HR practitioners have a secondary supportive partnering role. Could it be that as a result the HR function should not take a seat at the boardroom table because HR is no more than a support function, totally subordinate to their line leader business partners? In this chapter we would argue "no", that HR has a critical contribution to make to the organisation, one which it uniquely holds. However, to be effective in this role requires a paradigm shift from traditional HR practice. This shift is not so much in the area of "what we do," but rather "why we do it."

In Du Toit's doctoral research, completed in 2014,[145] this HR role was explored in detail, and some of the key findings of this research are reflected in this chapter. This chapter, which is more scientific in nature than the others, focuses on this role, its components, its potential impact and the capabilities and competencies required of HR practitioners as a result.

Context

In the corridors of the average HR departments I have worked with, there is a common, but private, view that line leadership just don't understand the "people" aspect of their jobs. It is tempting for HR practitioners to perceive and maintain a distance between their contribution to the "people" aspect of a business and that of their line colleagues. HR practitioners judge line leadership as follows: "Look at the impact of the latest line decision on morale, on labour turnover, on engagement, labour relations etcetera. If only they had consulted with us (HR) first."

We are challenging this perception with a very specific objective. As argued earlier in this book, organisational leadership transcends individual leadership relationships to the collective leadership culture. This can be seen in discussions in the lift club on the way to work, at the water fountain or around the canteen table, which start like this: "Can you believe it. **They** have now decided to cut bonuses?" These conversations happen whether we like it or not, on any given workday and across the organisation, even across the various levels the hierarchy. The "they" referred to in these discussions are the leadership of the organisation and how they are perceived, in other words the leadership culture.

Why is organisational leadership culture so important to HR?

Often the traditional HR focus on leadership has been on the development of leadership skills in young high-potential managers. While there is no disputing the fact that this is an important aspect of the HR development field, it is just a small aspect of the entire role that HR can potentially play in enabling an organisational leadership culture or brand.

Organisational leadership, and ultimately a leadership culture or brand, has the potential to impact directly on organisational competitiveness. There is a significant amount of research that demonstrates that effective leadership or the lack thereof plays a large role in ultimate organisational performance. Research shows that there is a direct relationship between effective leadership and the following:

- an organisation's financial performance[146]

- culture and cultural change[147]

- process improvement and project performance[148]

- the development of a high-performance work culture[149]

- improved organisational creativity and innovation[150]

- managing economic crises[151] and transmissions including mergers and acquisitions[152]

To some extent the research described above has focused on individual leadership. It is argued throughout this book that the benefits of creating an organisational leadership culture or even an externally recognised "organisational leadership brand" as proposed by Ulrich and Smallwood[153] have hugely significant potential value for the organisation.

This value may extend to impacting directly on organisational equity value. Examples of how building a leadership culture that is recognised by external stakeholders and thus extends organisational value are:

- the perception of the customer base ("I only bank at my bank because the bank I go to is so well run.")

- the value placed on the organisation by external business partners ("While we review all service contracts every three years, some providers are just run so well that this is merely a formality.")

- the decision to grow and develop a manufacturing base in a subsidiary of a multinational ("We awarded our South African auto-manufacturer the new product platform, because of the confidence head office has in the local company.")

- the decision to invest in equity by shareholders (one of the key determinants of potential equity growth examined by brokers is the quality of the leadership team. This also applies when a venture capital company acquires equity.)

- the bottom-line goodwill element on the balance sheet when assessing an organisation's market value (when evaluating a company's balance sheet, the item "goodwill" reflects the quality of leadership to a significant degree.)

This chapter is based on research conducted amongst HR practitioners in South Africa. This research found significant evidence that HR is in the space of building and growing leadership culture and brand and that a proactive HR department has the ability to uniquely and significantly impact on our future organisations. Leadership (culture and brand) beyond individual leadership relationships is, we believe, an area where HR can add great value in the future. To release this value requires a shift in thinking by the HR practitioner and, to a lesser degree, the organisation.

To illustrate this shift in thinking:

Consider Tony Nadal. He is Raffa Nadal's uncle. At the time of writing, Raffa Nadal is number one on the world tennis rankings. Tony Nadal is also Raffa's coach. While I'm sure Tony plays a great game of tennis himself, how does he get to coach the greatest tennis player on the global circuit? He never was, and never will be, as good a player as Raffa.

There is however one thing that Tony can do that Raffa will never be able to do – a unique contribution to their partnership. While Raffa's skills and experience allow him to assess any opponent and detect and exploit the vulnerability in his opponent's game, the one thing he cannot see, and will never be able to see, is himself. That is Tony's unique but critical role. He is the mirror, the reflection, the critic and the inspiration. He creates the environment in which Raffa is able to thrive.

This is the unique space that we believe the future HR function will increasingly be called to fill. The importance of this role must be seen in the context of the importance of a leadership culture, and ultimately a leadership brand, to organisation value.

This emerging HR role can be described as "creating a leadership brand enabling environment" or "an environment where line leadership thrives". This role will significantly challenge the traditional HR roles and competencies. The challenge is not so much that the HR environment will require new unique HR competencies, but rather that HR practitioners will need to re-examine their primary purpose – the **why**. When we really understand the **why**, we can integrate HR best practices in order to achieve a specific objective. This objective can be described as creating an environment where leadership thrives, an environment where authentic leadership culture emerges, a culture that is highly valued by external stakeholders, a "leadership brand".

The differences between leadership, leadership culture and leadership brand

A leadership brand has three levels, as illustrated in figure 5.1. Employees within an enterprise recognise both their individual leaders' brands and the collective leadership of an organisation. The collective practice of leadership constitutes an organisation's leadership culture. When an organisation's leadership culture is externally recognised by its stakeholders, this constitutes a leadership brand.

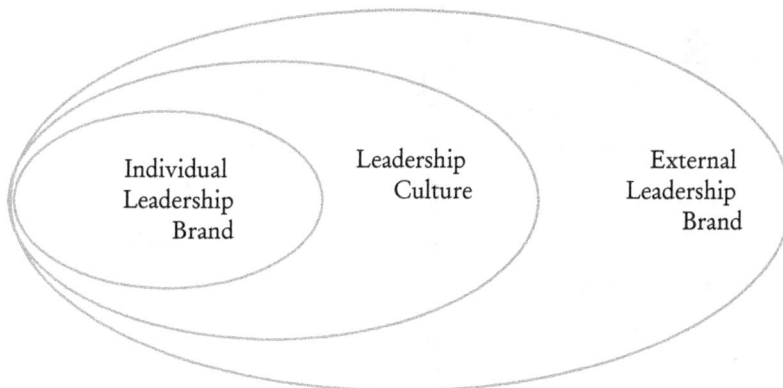

Figure 5.1 The three components of a leadership brand

The literature shows that an organisation's value is partly linked to the investment that stakeholders are prepared to make in the organisation, based on their valuation of the enterprise or the enterprise brand. To a large degree, the literature also shows that this enterprise brand is the product of a leadership brand. The quality of an organisation's leadership and its ability to create an effective and collective leadership culture determine the strength of the leadership brand, provided that the brand is recognised and valued by the organisation's stakeholders. The question is: how is this value achieved? Or, put differently, what would enable a leadership brand, the value of which is recognised by an organisation's stakeholders, to emerge? The next section focuses on identifying leadership brand enablers.

Leadership brand enablers

Not unlike astrology, in which when the "stars align" then great things happen, for a leadership culture and in particular a leadership brand to emerge, a wide range of activities and role-players need to act together. Figure 5.2 describes the various levels and role-players that, when functioning together, enable the emergence of a leadership brand.

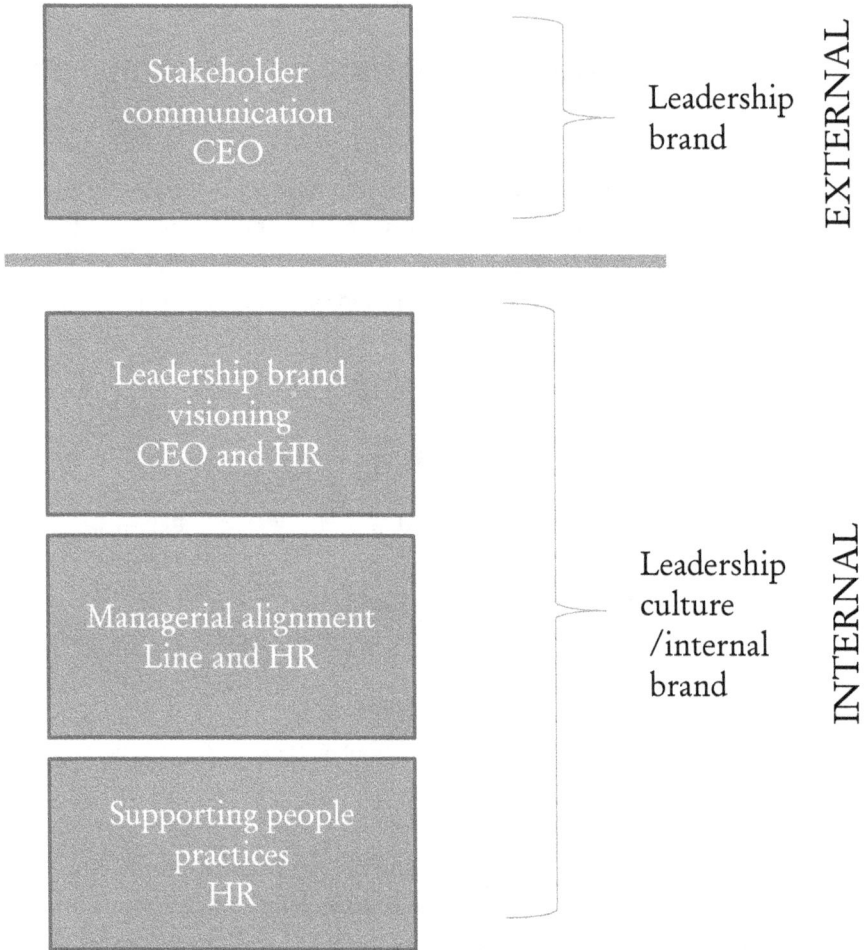

Figure 5.2 The different role-players required to enable a leadership brand

Figure 5.2 illustrates that in order to enable a leadership brand, the various organisational role-players have to make contributions at different levels, both internally and externally. The leadership brand enablers reported in this chapter were derived from a number of literature sources.[154] We identified the following enablers as important contributors.

A brief discussion of each enabler

As illustrated in figure 5.2, the enablers that allow a leadership culture and ultimately a leadership brand to emerge in an organisation originate from a variety of sources. In the research I conducted, the role of the CEO's enablement of a leadership brand was found to be one of the most crucial elements. Of the sample, 47 per cent reported that having stability in the CEO was one of the top three factors in the development of a leadership culture. This emphasises the importance of the CEO's role in the enablement of a leadership brand. However, while this is not an unexpected result, the role of the HR department in leadership brand enablement was also found to be critically important. A brief review of the various enablers identified above follows.

External – stakeholder level enablers

In order for a leadership brand to emerge, external recognition by the organisation's stakeholders is what differentiates a leadership brand from a leadership culture. This external communication of a leadership culture is a key part of the role of the CEO. The HR practitioner at executive level is further able to assist in the wider communication of the brand. The research conducted found that the importance of the CEO's alignment with the leadership brand and his or her communication thereof, both through public platforms and as an authentic example, are key for the translation of the brand, both externally and internally. The HR head can play a significantly important role in reflecting back to the CEO the CEO's alignment with the brand in action. However, the ability of the HR head to do this is to a large extent limited or improved by the practitioner's own credibility, as well as the practitioner's trust in the CEO. A CEO who is fully committed to and lives out a leadership brand is a key enabler of that leadership brand.

Internal – leadership brand visioning

To enable the emergence of a leadership brand, it is imperative that at the executive level of an organisation, a shared leadership brand vision emerges. The development of such a vision could be initiated by a range of different processes: however it is possible that the HR practitioner has a significant role to play in supporting such a vision development.

Some of the processes used to develop a shared vision could include executive conferences, workshops, expert input or other HR-facilitated opportunities. Ultimately though, a CEO's personal commitment to, drive towards and authentically living out a leadership vision in practice are key enablers of a leadership brand.

Internal – management and HR alignment

Once a leadership vision has been established, the commitment of the CEO to this vision and the alignment of management are crucial if an internal authentic leadership culture is to emerge. Some of the areas where the CEO is able to enhance this alignment are:

- the communication of the brand and its importance
- focusing on leadership as a personal responsibility
- personally demonstrated commitment to the leadership brand
- driving accountability
- supporting investment in leadership and monitoring the returns
- making the future leadership bench an area of personal focus

Ulrich and Smallwood[155] illustrate the "logic of leadership brand alignment", as shown in figure 5.3.

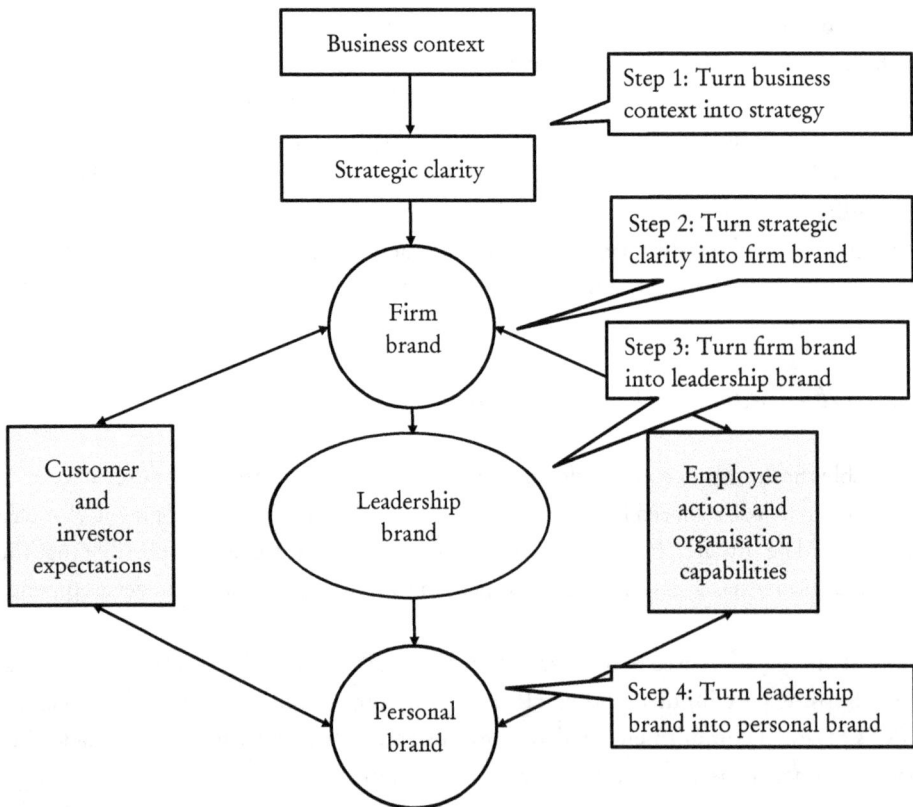

Figure 5.3 The alignment of strategy with leadership brand

Figure 5.3 shows how a leadership brand flows from an organisation's strategy and the enterprise brand it envisages establishing. The idea of an enterprise brand vs a product brand is increasingly being recognised as a key business asset. Where an enterprise brand answers the question "What does this organisation wish to be known for?", the leadership brand answers the question "How do we wish our organisation's leadership to be perceived externally?" This relies on the establishment of a clear vision of the desired "organisational leadership culture".

In some organisations this process emerges almost instinctively. However in most cases it may be necessary for the HR function to assist the CEO in creating and refining the leadership culture in the minds of line management. Ultimately the leadership culture needs to extend, be understood and be demonstrated across all levels of management. Mott and McLaughlin[156] provide an illustration of this in practice.

> Fiona Macleod Butts, director of talent at Southwest, said, "You could probably stop any of our leaders in the hall and say, 'What are our leadership expectations?' and they could recite them to you: 'The warrior's spirit, servant's heart, fun-loving attitude. Build great teams, think strategically and get excellent results.' That's our Leadership brand, and it is very well understood."

In the research conducted, it was found that in many organisations the HR department did not feel empowered to play this role. This just re-emphasises the crucial role the CEO plays in the enablement of a leadership brand. Where an organisation has an established leadership brand vision and where the CEO has empowered the HR function to play a leadership brand enabling role, it becomes possible for the HR function to contribute significantly to the growth of an authentic leadership culture. This HR role we call the "HR leadership brand enablement role".

As discussed in the introduction to this chapter, this role creates an opportunity for the HR function to make a significant contribution to the organisation, beyond the current HR business partner role.

Internal – supporting people practices

From the literature and the research conducted, 11 HR leadership brand enablers were identified. The role of the HR department in leadership brand enablement was found to be one of the three most important roles the HR practitioner can fulfil.

However the real secret to HR playing a significant "leadership brand enabling role" does not lie in the individual enablers themselves, but in the integration of all these diverse activities into a coherent and integrated HR strategy – a strategy which has as its essence the enablement of the leadership culture. As a result, it is important to note at this stage that the capability and competence of the HR practitioner is critical. This will determine to what extent each of these enablers is integrated into a holistic coherent leadership brand enablement strategy.

In this section we briefly touch on each one of the HR leadership brand enablers. The elements of HR competency and capability are discussed in more detail later in this section.

HR leader alignment

In order for a leadership brand culture to develop within an organisation, the HR practitioners and in particular senior executives need to display personal commitment and alignment to the leadership culture. HR executives have a significant responsibility to be the embodiment of the leadership culture. This requires in practice an authentic alignment in their daily activities, and the demonstration of exceptional leadership commitment.

In practice, consider the message conveyed by the standards set for basic HR practice. For example, performance management and talent acquisition are not maintained by the HR functional head. The old idea that "the dentist's kids have the worst teeth" immediately undermines the authenticity of a leadership culture.

Facilitation of the establishment of a leadership brand

The responsibility for determining the need for and establishing the vision of what constitutes a leadership brand was described as a CEO responsibility. But the responsibility of the CEO relies on the facilitation skills often developed in HR management. HR leaders can play a significant role in helping facilitate the brand establishment.

Cohen and Sinha[157] describe this as follows: "Once you have consensus that the organisation wants to have a Leadership brand, deciding on the right brand is the critical first step. Learning leaders (HR) should bring together leaders from across the organisation to answer the question: 'What do we want to be known for?'"

A communication process which engages stakeholders in the leadership brand is key to its emergence.

Assessment

Organisations use a wide range of assessment processes and tools. The purpose of these tools can range from the assessment of new hire capability, the current talent pool, or the organisational culture and employee engagement. Providing effective assessment instruments is part of HR work. Without trying to prescribe specific assessment processes, the shift in thinking for the HR practitioner in leadership brand enablement is significant. Again it concerns the question: why are we doing this assessment? For leadership brand enablement the HR practitioner needs to ensure that all assessment activities across the organisation (of individual, current and future talent and organisational culture) shift from just considering job performance, competency and capability to leadership brand alignment.

Ulrich and Smallwood[158] stress the importance of aligning competency models and the assessment of leaders with a leadership brand. Beyond standard assessment approaches, they include input into the assessment process by stakeholders – either directly or through surveys.[159]

Assessment in this context should include multiple-level assessment of internal and external perceptions. There is a real danger that assessment of top leadership's perceptions of the leadership culture may not be the same as assessment of employees' or stakeholders' perceptions.

In order to enable the leadership development process to support a leadership brand, the leadership alignment to the brand must be constantly assessed. Such assessment should range from feedback loops to formal assessment processes. Also refer to chapter 6, where we unpack leadership talent assessment in more detail.

Coaching leaders

Coaching is an important tool used by HR leaders. In the context of establishing a leadership brand, coaching can be used and encouraged throughout the organisation.

Ulrich and Beatty[160] suggest the following: "In coaching executives, one can begin with an examination of the stakeholder relationships to understand the executives' goals with each stakeholder, how these relate to each other in the firm's business model, and how to measure attainment of the goals."

Ulrich and Johnson identify two focal points for coaching organisational leaders: behavioural change and strategy realisation. The first focuses on correcting behaviour and the second focuses on clarifying business strategy. There are five potential sources of coaching in organisations:

- self-coaching achieved through personal reflection
- peer coaching using internal colleagues who can be trusted
- peer coaching by using professional networks
- coaching by the leader
- expert coaching, using a professionally appointed external coach[161]

In the context of the leadership brand, the coaching process should be part of a comprehensive strategy with the leadership culture and brand in mind, and not just a stand-alone initiative.

Succession planning

The concept of building an effective leadership pipeline has been promoted by Charan et al.[162] They stress that there is a need for organisations to manage the leadership pipeline in order to ensure a continuous flow of adequately skilled leaders through an organisation. The "pipeline" they propose recognises the different levels of leadership within an organisation and the need for organisations to have focused programmes to ensure that leaders move through them. Succession is so important in creating a leadership brand that Ulrich and Smallwood[163] suggest that leaders should be assessed in terms of "their contribution to – or consumption of – the talent."

In my research the importance of leadership having the complexity-generating capability appropriate for their level emerged as a crucial element. This is briefly discussed later in this chapter, but in summary there is significant evidence that while we can develop leaders to lead more effectively, the leader's ability to manage at a certain level of complexity is largely part of the individual's inherent capability.

In practice we all instinctively know that this is true. For instance, we are well aware that the best nursing sister may not necessary be a great matron, the best teacher a great principal or the best researcher and lecturer the best faculty head.

In developing an effective leadership pipeline, the HR practitioner will need to integrate the assessment of capability with the other elements of succession planning. The enablement of a leadership brand requires an organisational succession-planning process, which ensures a pipeline of capable talent prepared to support the future of the leadership brand.

Training and leadership development

There are many leadership development programmes available today. What differentiates training and development strategies in a leadership brand context from traditional strategies is the link to the influence of external stakeholders and the way training value is assessed. In the leadership brand context, leadership training should not be focused on the individual, but rather on building organisational leadership capacity.

Ulrich and Smallwood[164] ask: "If your best customers or investors could observe the training you offer your company leaders, how would they respond? Would they see the development of leaders who have the knowledge and skills to meet their requirements? Or would they see training that is perfunctory and has little to do with their needs and desires?"

Effective HR practitioners traditionally do a gap analysis when considering an organisational learning strategy. A gap analysis requires the careful and structured assessment of the level of current organisationally critical competencies against a vision of what level would be ideal to support future business directions. Such practitioners are not influenced by attractive training offerings presented off-the-shelf in the marketplace, but rather on initiatives which address identified organisational needs.

To build a leadership brand effectively, training and learning strategies, and in particular leadership development activities, must be integrated. Some of the considerations that emerge in this context are:

- the use of leaders as teachers
- the use of customers as teachers
- experiences and exposure as key learning and development tools
- investing in the collective leadership code
- focus on the organisation's key result areas and its core competencies as a priority
- the importance of aligning learning and development with business strategy
- clarity about role or level expectations

Ultimately learning and development is a key tool for enabling a successful leadership culture and brand. However, it is never an activity in itself but part of a total collective strategy. The investment in learning and development cannot be fully realised, and falls into a vacuum, unless the other HR enablers are in place. This again places emphasis on the leadership brand enabling role as a core HR role, which spans the practice of effective HR.

Performance management

An effective performance management system is one of the enablers required to develop a leadership brand-aligned leadership team or pipeline. The entire leadership of an organisation should be involved in identifying and managing the performance of leadership as people progress through the pipeline.

HR practitioners need to be very mindful that performance management systems don't always have a good reputation in organisations. They can be a threatening experience and often require onerous administration. Often the recommendations and development activities identified during this process are not followed up.

What is recommended in this context is a not a stand-alone process which focuses on determining increases in remuneration. In building a leadership brand enabling environment, the performance management system is a continuous process, one which is fully integrated with all the other HR activities necessary to build a leadership pipeline.

Recognition

In leadership brand enablement, traditional recognition systems need to be changed from a pure results focus (what was achieved) to a focus on the effectiveness of leadership collaboration (how it was achieved). Hernez-Broome and Hughes believe that organisations wishing to develop a strong leadership culture "will also need to be the kind of organisations that nurture and reinforce enactment of the kinds of behaviours desired in those leaders".[165]

A recognition system which recognises and rewards leadership brand competencies and alignment is important for the emergence of a leadership brand.

HR policies

On a fundamental level, HR leaders, through the way that they shape the policies and practices of HR throughout the employee lifecycle, can ensure that HR practices reflect the desired leadership brand and connect customer expectations with employee actions. As leaders are required to operate within HR policies, it is critically important that policies reinforce the leadership brand and don't undermine it. HR policies first and foremost need to empower and guide line leadership, and not impede its ability to lead.

Recruitment

In the context of leadership brand enablement, the importance of maintaining a link between the recruitment and selection of staff and corporate brand values is paramount.

The role of recruitment in the creation of a specific culture is perhaps best described by Collins,[166] in his famous comment on recruitment: "But I know this much: If we get the right people on the bus, the right people in the right seats, and the wrong people off the bus, then we'll figure out how to take it some place great."

When it comes to leadership recruitment, three key components of HR's leadership brand enablement role must be considered.

- The public advertising of the position is a "letter of intent" to external stakeholders and an essential part of branding. For instance, how you position your organisation during graduate recruitment may reinforce or undermine external recognition of the intended leadership brand.

- When appointing leadership, the capability of the leader must transcend job competencies, and this may create a challenge for the HR practitioner. Line leadership are naturally impressed by candidates who will produce business results quickly, whereas the ability to align the company's leadership brand is equally uncompromising.

- Through the introduction and induction process the HR practitioner has a unique opportunity to influence the new leader, ensuring that he or she is leadership brand-aligned in practice from the outset. This is far easier to achieve at entry than over time.

Thus a recruitment process which attracts leadership capable of aligning with the leadership brand is a key enabler of leadership culture development.

Summary of leadership brand enablers

The HR enablers described above have been taken from the literature and categorised into a new HR role – leadership brand enablement. All these enablers, irrespective of the approach or even the degree to which they have been implemented, do not amount to a leadership brand by themselves. Where an organisation has embarked on a strategy to develop a leadership brand, the potential for a significant HR role – the HR leadership brand enablement role – emerges. My research showed that this role is easily recognised by HR practitioners of varied degrees of capability.

This recognition was specifically identified through a rank order process. Using Ulrich, Younger, Brokbank and Ulrich's[167] HR competency clusters as a framework, the sample was requested to rank their competency clusters/roles in order of importance. The HR leadership brand enablement role discussed above was added to this list and the findings are reflected in figure 5.4. The HR leadership brand enablement role was identified as being the third most important role.

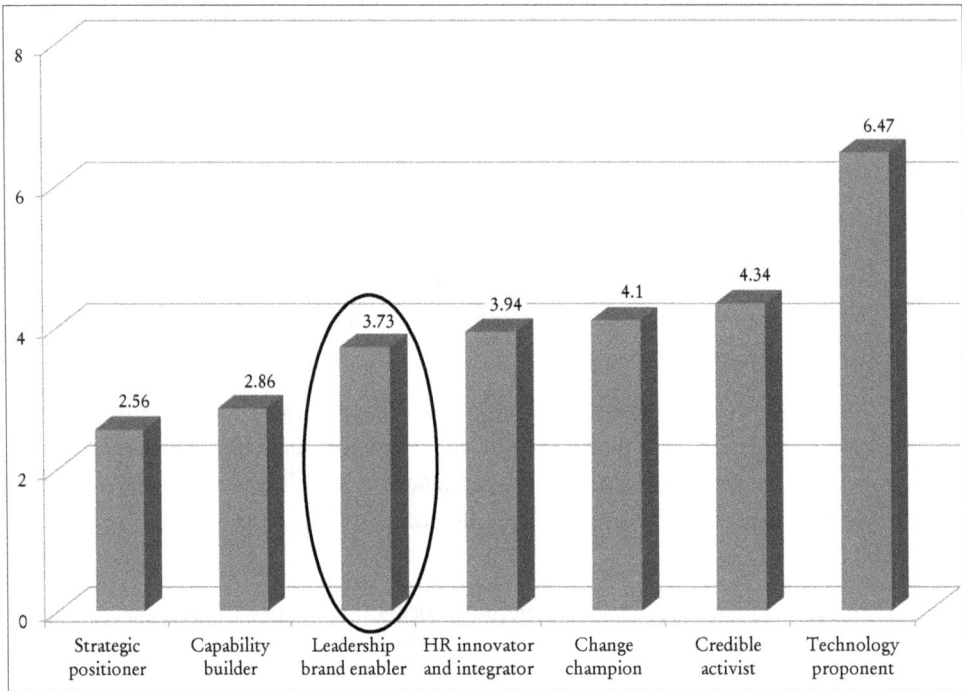

Figure 5.4 HR roles ranked in order of importance

While this provided solid evidence that HR practitioners could identify this role and in fact gave it significant priority, it did not show whether HR practitioners possessed the requisite competencies and capabilities to fill this role. This is discussed in the next section, as there is a significant difference between recognising a role and being able to perform it.

Conclusion

While the role of strategic business partner has become a key standard HR practitioner role, there still appears to be some debate on whether this role justifies the HR chair having a seat at the boardroom table. This chapter does not discount the need for HR practitioners to partner with line leadership around the people dynamic. However, it proposes that there is a more complex role which if fully actualised by the HR function would create a unique space for the HR function to directly impact on organisational value.

This role, the HR leadership brand enabling role, was easily recognised by the HR practitioners surveyed, although very few felt empowered to explore its potential. This limitation could have a number of sources, from a lack of understanding about the importance of leadership culture and brand by the CEO, to a limitation in the personal capability of the HR practitioner to create a fully integrated enablement environment.

The ability of HR to open up this unique area of contribution relies heavily on a number of key factors:

1. the total support for and drive behind the establishment of a leadership culture by the CEO

2. a clear articulation of a leadership brand

3. a paradigm shift from the purpose behind traditional HR practice towards creating an environment where leaders thrive

4. the full integration of core HR functions into a single strategy to create a leadership brand enabling environment

5. HR practitioners with adequate competencies having an effect on each function

6. most importantly, HR practitioners and especially the HR head having sufficient capability in terms of complexity generation

Can HR make a significant contribution to organisational performance and effectiveness and ultimately the value of the organisation, as described by its external shareholders and stakeholders? We believe it can, but this will require a significant shift from traditional HR practice. It will require that HR practitioners embrace the idea that line leaders are ultimately responsible for employees. **However, HR is responsible for creating an enabling environment where line leaders thrive.**

Chapter 6

Spotting leadership talent

Letitia van der Merwe

Contributing author: Ronel Minnaar

❄

"We need leaders and not just political leaders. We need leaders in every field, in every institution, in all kinds of situations. We need to be educating our young people to be leaders. And unfortunately, that's fallen out of fashion."
– American historian David McCullough

"I have known talented people who procrastinate indefinitely rather than risk failure." **– Charles Stanley**

Everyone liked the candidate

"It happened again," Ted explained. "I told myself that the next time we needed to hire someone, I would be prepared for the interview."

"And?" I asked.

"Scott came down the hallway. He said the candidate in the conference room had talked to four other people and everyone liked him. Heck, I didn't even know we had interviews scheduled.

"He asked if I had fifteen minutes to talk to the candidate, just to see if I liked him, too. Funny, I liked him, too."

"So, what's the problem?" I pursued.

"Everyone liked him, but here we are, two months down the road and I find out he doesn't have any experience in one of the most critical parts of the job. He just told me point blank that he has never done this before. Worst part, he tells me he doesn't even see that as part of his job. If we need that done, he suggests we hire an expert or a consultant to help out.

Source: http://managementblog.org/author/fosterlearning/

It is so easy to get leadership talent identification wrong. Spotting leadership talent is a minefield, as it is cluttered with our own perceptions and biases around what we think good leadership means.

The story so far and the link to leadership talent

In **chapter 1** we shared interesting and very important views which impact on how organisations should approach spotting leadership talent. Leadership is more and more seen as a social process that engages everyone in the community. However, organisations have traditionally been and still are focused on developing individuals so that they can become better leaders; they put the emphasis on individual learning through the concepts of leader development and individual development plans. There seems to be a growing recognition that the emphasis should be on developing leadership as a collective. We envisage that the future will very likely be about developing leadership communities and networks of leaders, and therefore when spotting and developing leadership talent it clearly does not make sense to focus only on the individual. The future challenge is to create a community of leaders able and willing to lead organisations through the turbulence of an increasingly complex world.

Chapter 2 proposed a new leadership landscape. We suggest a much stronger relationship between social patterns and trends and the nature of leadership and the notion that "the leader" be supplemented with an equally strong focus on "leadership community". It is our view that the leadership of an organisation forms a community of practice with its own ideology, beliefs, value set and code of practice. Secondly, a certain leadership culture is associated with the leadership community – the interpersonal, team, and organisation-wide dynamics amongst the organisation's leadership. Organisations aiming to improve their approach to spotting leadership talent will have to take these shifts in the leadership landscape into consideration.

In **chapter 3** we found ourselves in unchartered waters, as there is very little formal writing about leadership community. We describe "leadership community" as the leaders at all levels of the organisation who consciously share a common purpose and who have a high degree of congruence, not only on the **how** of achieving the purpose, but also and more importantly the **why**. The implications for leadership community shared in this chapter must be taken into consideration when spotting leadership talent. The existence of leadership community depends on the decisions taken at an organisational level as well as the choices and decisions of individuals. A very important requirement is not only whether an individual has acquired all the competencies and skills required to fulfil the role of a leader, but whether the individual has the dexterity (agility) to deal with strategic, emotional and change-related aspects.

The key implication in **chapter 4** is that we need to remember that leaders are people too. We should not be looking for heroic acts by individuals who "know best" and "know it all" in order to save the organisation. We need to realise that not all leadership is good for the organisation. We need to identify those individuals who are able to operate in the context of people, the business, the industry and the larger social environment. Secondly, it is not about finding the "ideal leader", but rather those individuals who are self-aware, authentic and continuously strive to be the best leader they can be.

In **chapter 5** we explored the envisaged and proposed changes to the role HR practitioners should play within their organisations. We certainly believe that HR can make a significant contribution to organisational performance and effectiveness. For this to happen, HR practitioners must embrace the idea that leaders are ultimately responsible for employees and that their responsibility is to create the enabling environment where line leaders thrive. In most instances spotting leadership talent is seen as a key value contribution HR makes to the organisation. The key implication for spotting talent potential is therefore that HR practices need to fully align with the leadership brand strategy and values transcendence – from individual leadership relationships to a collective leadership culture.

The objective of this chapter is to pull together these key messages and their implications for spotting leadership talent. We explore what leadership talent is and what the key attributes are. We also share key aspects to take into consideration when spotting leadership talent and redefining the approach. Lastly, we propose a leadership transitioning process as a means of ensuring integrated talent management and development that will produce extraordinary results for the individual as well as the organisation.

Important considerations for spotting leadership talent

In a world that is complex, uncertain and fast-paced, finding true talent that is capable of dealing with such volatility and complexity is key. Within these complex and ever-changing organisational contexts, finding and developing leadership talent has become much more than an empty buzzword; it has become a strategic and operational tool for achieving results.

According to the CEO Challenge 2014, a survey of CEOs, presidents and chairpersons from more than 1 000 companies around the world, the most pressing challenge their businesses were facing in the year ahead is how to best develop, engage, manage and retain talent.

The Corporate Leadership Council found in their 2010 research that best-in-class leadership talent strategies are aligned with organisational strategy and are also based on rigorous leadership talent and needs analysis. This means that in order for the organisation to build an effective leadership community a long-term view is required. Identifying and defining critical leadership capabilities and risks must be based on strategic priorities and should not focus on current leadership needs alone.

At a recent round table conversation with clients and partners, some key considerations for identifying leadership talent were shared:

- Define a clear leadership philosophy and purpose before identifying leaders.
- Use the strategy to guide the definition of leadership talent.
- Be clear about what leadership must drive, namely culture and results.
- Constantly check the purpose and process of leadership development against the organisation's strategy.
- Define what future talent is and be clear about what is nonnegotiable.
- Talent identification and development processes should allow for "ideal" diversity and not just diversity for the sake of being diverse.

According to a working paper published by INSEAD in 2010, the authors Manfred Kets de Vries and Konstantin Korotov[168] concluded that as the world is changing, leadership can no longer be defined by what a single leader does. Leadership needs to be defined by the ability to collaborate, motivate and manage networks. According to the authors, a distributed view of leadership is on the rise. The focus needs to shift away from the traditional single leader to an intricate and complex community of leaders who possess a range of abilities and experiences necessary to ensure that the leadership function is carried out to the benefit of the wider organisation.

With these changes to leadership and how it needs to be redefined, surely the way in which companies approach the identification and nurturing of leadership talent should also change?

Redefining our approach to identifying and nurturing talent

David Clutterbuck[169] introduced the idea of a "talent wave", noting that "talent" is dynamic, complex and energetic – it needs to be harnessed, not controlled – hence the concept of a "wave" as opposed to a pool (static) or pipeline (linear). The assumption is that a dynamic talent wave is ever-changing and one in which people work towards bettering themselves.

Business organisations can be described as open social systems that are constantly in interaction with a broader society, simultaneously shaping and being shaped by broader social forces. If we support the notion that organisations are actually complex adaptive systems, then what Clutterbuck is suggesting actually makes a lot of sense: we cannot and should not look at talent management from a linear perspective any more.

There are a number of myths organisations believe about talent which need to be discarded:

- If we assess and develop talent we will be all right.

- Past performance is a predictor of performance in a more complex role.

- Talent is only about success and exceptional achievement.

- You can "microwave" talented people to make them ready quicker.

Organisations identify talent based on a combination of desired or ideal criteria related to the job profile. Some of these criteria have included physical attributes (where applicable), intelligence, experience, past performance, competencies, characteristics, skills and knowledge. Increasingly, organisations find that these criteria are no longer effective predictors of successful performance.

Claudio Fernández-Aráoz,[170] in a recent *Harvard Business Review* article titled *21st Century Talent Spotting*, suggests that in a volatile, uncertain, complex and ambiguous environment, the focus when identifying talent should move towards potential, as competency-based assessments are increasingly inadequate. He considers potential to be the most important predictor of success at all levels, from junior management to the C-suite executive and the board. Potential is defined as the ability to adapt to and grow into increasingly complex roles and environments.

As business becomes more volatile and complex, and the global market for top professionals gets tougher, organisations and their leaders must transition to a new era of talent spotting, where evaluations are based on potential instead of brawn, brains, experience or competencies. The new question to ask is not whether the company's employees and leaders have the right skills; it's whether they have the potential to learn new ones.

What is leadership talent and what are the key attributes?

The idea of an "ideal profile" is becoming outdated as quickly as organisational contexts change. In our experience, the conversations around talent identification and development have also changed. Organisations are trying to understand what future talent will look like and what they really need to focus on to build the best future leaders for their organisations.

Leadership talent means different things at different levels of the organisation. We argue that leadership talent should not refer to the "select few" high-potential leaders who will become the next CEO, director or executive in the company. Yes, this is critically important, but so is the employee who will become the next supervisor, middle manager and senior manager. We need to spot, nurture and position talent for the entire leadership community.

Various contributors and writers of leadership blogs share the view that more than talent is required of individuals to become leaders in the first place. Leadership is not only about skills and talents; it is about a journey filled with personal character development, personal growth and the ability to display agility.

John C Maxwell[171] reminds us that it is very important for a leader to get the right people in the organisation and put them in the right positions. In his book *Leadership Gold*, one of the chapters – "Don't send your ducks to eagle school" – caught our attention. We share some extracts which in our view are very applicable here. According to Maxwell, good people are found, not changed. They can change themselves, but we as leaders cannot change them. If we want good people we have to find them. Leadership is all about placing people in the right place so they can be successful. Leaders need to know and value their people for who they are and let them work according to their strengths.

According to Maxwell, our ability to grow and change is very different depending on whether or not we can make choices. Our growth potential is unlimited in the areas of attitude, character and responsibility; these can be improved by making the right choices. Natural ability, and according to our definition capability, is not a choice, it is a gift; people have whatever they have.

He continues that leaders' responsibility is to know what they are looking for. Leaders need to know what qualities and characteristics are present in leaders who are successful in their industry.

As the notion of having an "ideal profile" to use for spotting talent is becoming outdated, what are those attributes companies need to focus on in order to spot the right leadership talent that will address the company's current and future needs?

> Strategic agility is the ability to continuously adjust and adapt the strategic direction in core business, and to create not just new products and services, but also new business models and innovative ways to create value for the company.
>
> **Yves Doz and Mikko Kosonen**

What we are experiencing is that the demand for leadership is moving away from isolated behavioural competencies toward complex "thinking" abilities. These manifest as adaptive competencies such as learning agility, self-awareness, comfort with ambiguity and strategic thinking. The demanding and complex business world requires leadership that is able to create shared possible futures and realise a shared, specific chosen future with, through and for people. Leadership is seen more and more as a social process that engages everyone in the community.

Recent research conducted by INSEAD[172] highlights the importance of strategic agility. According to the authors Yves Doz and Mikko Kosonen,[173] companies' traditional response to change through strategic planning no longer fits because change is fast and unpredictable. Also, globalisation gave rise to trade and investment liberalisation and companies competing for access to global resources and pockets of knowledge and know-how to enable their innovations. We need to identify leaders with strategic agility.

According to an article by the John Maxwell Company written in 2013,[174] a common set of characteristics shared by great leaders throughout history is character, perspective, courage and favour. Without character, a leader is unstable and prone to moral failure. There are plenty of examples of talented people who sabotaged their careers by abandoning their values. Character sustains excellence over time and the absence of strong character eventually topples talent. Without perspective a leader has no sense of direction. Without courage a leader cowers at the sight of a big challenge, and without favour a leader cannot persuade others to take action.

The CEO Challenge 2014 conducted by the Conference Board also highlights that ethical working is high on the agenda, with CEOs rating integrity as the most important leadership attribute. The remainder of the top five leadership attributes were leading change, managing complexity, an entrepreneurial mindset and the ability to retain and develop talent.

We define capability as "the ability to generate, prefer and demonstrate appropriate work-type specific complexity, values, activities, perception, judgement, interpersonal qualities, problem solving, etcetera. Capability refers to those aspects of a person that are inherently part of him/her and which cannot be changed or developed (trained) easily".[175] We are of the view that this ability to generate and work with complexity, especially in the complex business environments in which leaders function, is of particular importance.

Another key attribute to consider in the new landscape of talent spotting is a leader's agility profile. Lominger International defines learning agility as a construct supported by four subdimensions: mental agility, people agility, change agility and results agility.[176] Our representation of how these four subdimensions relate to learning agility is depicted in figure 6.1.

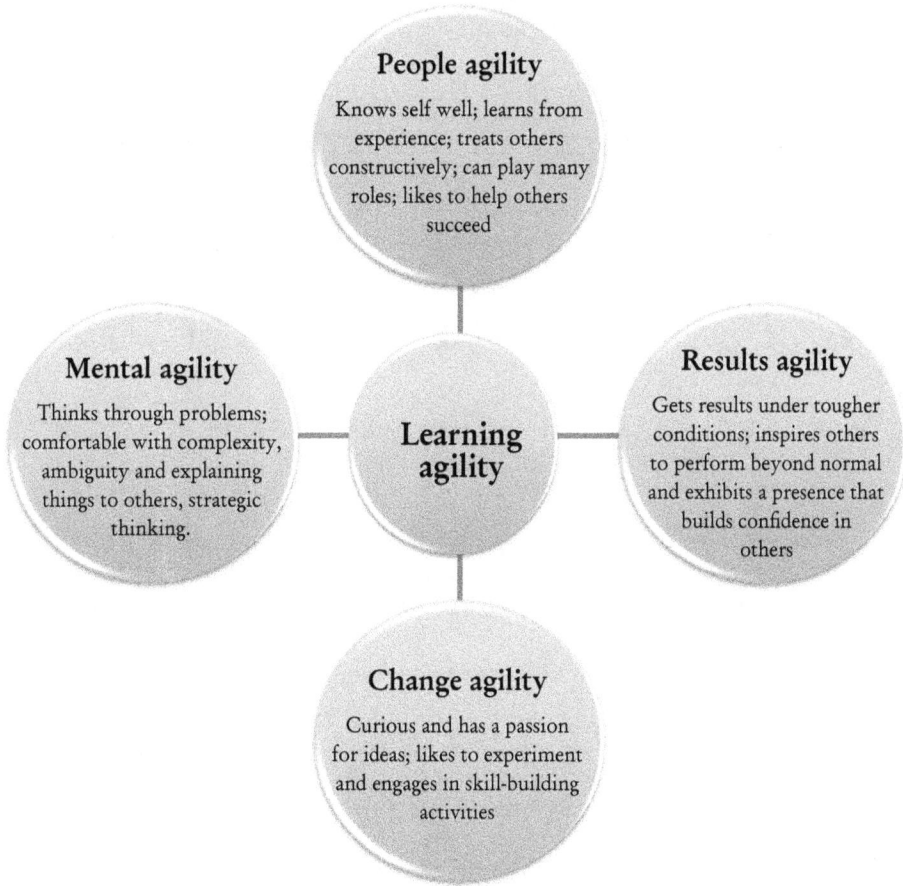

Figure 6.1 The Lominger learning agility dimensions

The leader's ability to be self-aware and have self-insight is also seen as a key capability. It is our view that self-awareness and self-insight are made possible through four dimensions: character development, integrity, emotional intelligence and personal ownership. Our representation of how these four dimensions relate to self-awareness and self-insight is depicted in figure 6.2.

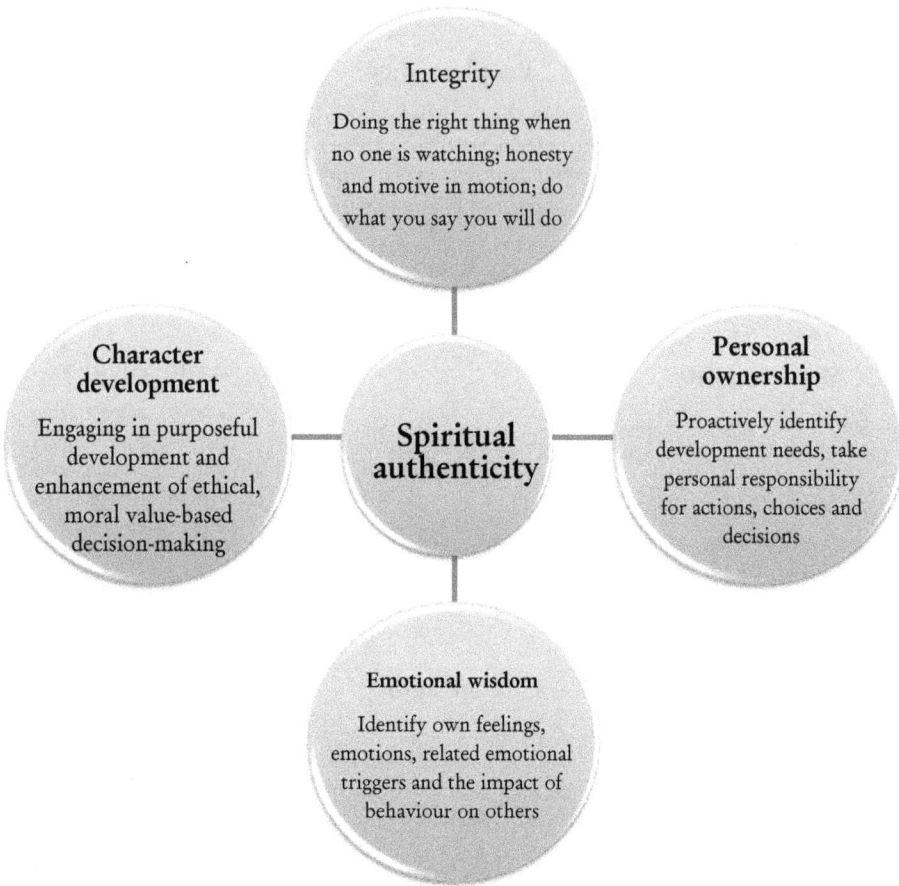

Figure 6.2 Self-awareness and self-insight

It is our conclusion that a leader's capability, agility profile and spiritual authenticity, along with the necessary technical know-how, are critical attributes to consider in the quest for true leadership talent.

What we are suggesting is that talent should not be seen as two-dimensional (performance vs potential) but more as something complex and evolving. Organisations should focus a lot more on making sense of their organisation's talent challenges and developing a richer form of talent intelligence.

Nurturing leadership talent

Rebecca Ray, Senior Vice-President at the Conference Board and co-author of the report, is of the opinion that building a culture that supports engagement, employee training, leadership development, and high performance is something companies can control, and is making the difference between growing market share and simply surviving in 2014. Moreover, if the focus of individual companies is sustained, Human Capital may well be the engine that revives economic growth.[177]

The CEO Challenge 2014 findings also emphasise the importance of management performance, with improving leadership development programmes now ranked fifth globally and up five places from the previous year's survey. European CEOs place this factor at number one when it comes to strategies for building human capital.

For most participating CEOs the focus is on developing what is already in place, with nine out of the top 10 human capital strategies focusing on current employees, including providing training and development, raising employee engagement and increasing efforts to retain critical talent. Mirroring this, creating a strong internal talent pipeline (or in our view, talent waves) rather than seeking to recruit externally is considered a priority.

According to De Vries and Korotov,[178] leadership development cannot happen by chance if the standards of excellence and versatility for mastering today's complex business environment are to be achieved. Many senior executives still hold on to the idea that the HR department is primarily responsible for developing their organisation's future leaders. Leader development efforts that produce the best leaders are those in which senior leaders plan the initiative and take an active part as coaches, mentors, teachers and role models. Effective leadership is not just an event – it is an ongoing journey for both emerging leaders and senior management.

Organisations have traditionally focused on developing individuals so that they can become better leaders, which gave rise to the concept of leader development. They are of the opinion that it does not make sense for organisations to focus only on developing individual leaders. There is a growing recognition that the emphasis should be on developing leadership as a collective. They envisage that the future will very likely be about developing leadership communities and networks of leaders.

In our view, nurturing leadership talent should not follow a "one size fits all" approach, but rather a "fit-for-purpose approach" which works on an inside-out principle (eg intrapersonal, interpersonal, organisational and external community). The learning process must be collaborative in nature and include a development philosophy that allows for formal learning that is supported by reflection, coaching/mentoring and action learning, in order to create sustainable and transferable learning application in the workplace.

There is no doubt in our minds that nurturing the right leadership talent is a key priority for organisations. However, it is a concern that in many instances leadership development happens by chance and still follows a "one size fits all" approach. Data about employees becomes talent intelligence when more than just administrative information about an individual is gathered and stored.

Nik Kinley and Shlomo Ben-Hur[179] are of the opinion that the challenge most companies face is that their information about talent does not always provide the required intelligence when it comes to hiring, developing and promoting people. According to these authors, talent intelligence is the understanding organisations have of the skills, expertise and qualities of their people. Companies can only make good talent decisions if they know what they need, what they have and what is available.

Talent intelligence therefore enables organisations to make deliberate choices about proactively attracting the right talent and developing this talent to address current and future needs and requirements. Talent intelligence will also increase organisations' effectiveness in navigating leadership talent through the various transition phases, pacing individuals' readiness for placement for the shorter as well as the longer term.

Leadership transition

According to Charan et al,[180] the starting point for building the leadership base is to understand the natural hierarchy of work that exists in organisations. The focus is on managerial-leadership work rather than technical, administrative or professional work. This hierarchy takes the form of six career passages. Each passage represents a change in organisational position – a different level and complexity of leadership – where a significant transition has to be made. A transition from one career passage to another involves a major change in job requirements, demanding new skills, time applications and work values.

While times of transition can be exciting and energising, they often prove difficult for the leader who has a new role, as well as for the followers who experience changes in their environment. It is estimated that only 41 per cent of new-to-role managers make smooth transitions into their new roles, based on survey responses of the managers of new-to-role managers.

New leaders have a natural desire to make a unique contribution within the new role and to the organisation. Often, they feel the need to set themselves apart from the previous leader. As a result, the new leader often appears to take a critical stance toward current organisational processes and policies. He or she offers a suggestion for every issue that arises in an attempt to demonstrate his or her ability to contribute. Talented leaders are able to make a smooth transition into a more complex role and as a result, the need to "prove their ability" is less evident.

Transitions from one career passage to another require that leaders acquire a new way of managing and leading and that they leave the old way of doing behind. New capabilities are required to execute new responsibilities, new time frames govern how the leader needs to work and lastly, leaders are required to change what they believe is important, resulting in a shift in focus of their efforts.

Figure 6.3 is a conceptual representation of what is meant by leadership transitioning.

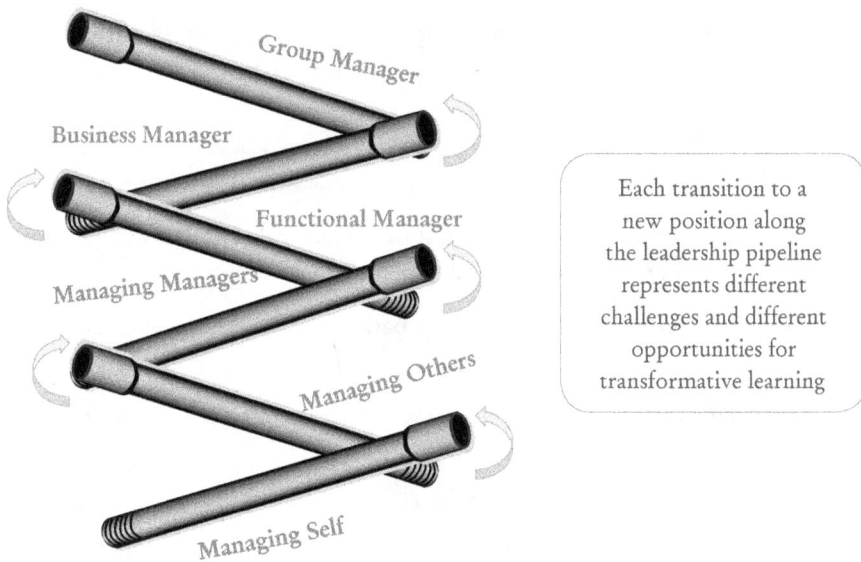

Each transition to a new position along the leadership pipeline represents different challenges and different opportunities for transformative learning

Figure 6.3 Leadership transitioning[181]

Transitions can vary on a number of dimensions which are not mutually exclusive.[182]

- Intensity: degree to which the new role requires new learning because it does not permit the exercise of prior knowledge, practised skills and established relationships

- **Surprise**: extent to which the actual experience is unexpected

- **Desirability**: extent to which the transition represents a progress/opportunity for diversity (ie high desirability), or a regression/adversity (ie low desirability)

- **Complexity**: increase in discretion of decision-making and judgement required[183]

The implications of leader transitions

Have you ever considered how long it takes a middle and/or senior manager in transition to reach the point where they become creators of value for their organisations? A survey of over 200 company CEOs and presidents yielded an estimate of 6.2 months for the typical new leader to reach this point of value-add and value creation.[184] Every leader in transition impacts – often negatively rather than positively – the performance of more than a dozen employees. It is therefore critical to understand the impact of leadership transitioning on the individual as well as on the organisation.

Impact on the individual

Research and our own experience reveal that a transitioning process has the following impact on the transitioning leader and those around him or her:

- **Transition failure:** Over 75 per cent of high-potential leaders experience moderate to significant problems when they move into a new role.[185]

- **Transition anxiety:** The ability to adjust to the new role requires different ways of thinking and doing, which often creates anxiety.

- **Dealing with failure:** This is inevitably part of the leadership journey and often assists in creating more successful leaders.

- **Being passed over for promotion:** Leaders often need to let go of their ambition, resulting in depression.

- **Losing faith in the system:** Often leaders lose faith in the business world, in their organisation and more specifically its senior leaders.

Some implications of the impact leadership transitions have on the leader and their environment are:

- **Sometimes leaders leave a "mess" behind:** When leadership transitions result in leaders being promoted too quickly, someone else needs to deal with the consequences of the decisions made by the leader who did not stay long enough to see his or her own decisions through to fruition.

- **"We were peers, now you are my leader":** This can be challenging for the new leader as well as those who have to adapt to their old colleague's new role and level of authority.

- **"A new broom sweeps clean" syndrome:** New leaders, driven by the belief that they need to prove themselves from a position of power, often tend to micromanage their direct reports.

Impact on the organisation

From an organisational perspective, ineffective management of leadership transitions often results in political interference, with conflicting interests and intrigue. Some other implications are:

- The consequences of making the "wrong" decision must be faced.

- Transition acceleration, often referred to as "fast-tracking", can result in individuals being promoted too quickly. This is also supported by a misplaced perspective that we can "microwave" an individual's skills, competence and capability and that individuals will "grow into the role over time".

- Talent retention: not everyone can be promoted, and a key consideration is how to retain those talented individuals who aren't promoted but are recognised as future talent. Expectations must be managed, especially those of talented individuals who believe they are not promoted "fast enough".

Possible solution

> If designed well the meshing of talent management and leadership development will produce extraordinary results for both the individual and the organisation.
>
> **Kets de Vries and Korotov**

According to Kets de Vries and Korotov,[186] organisations have always struggled with recruiting, retaining and developing high-quality people. A primarily challenge for nurturing and developing leadership talent is talent management.

It is therefore important that all talent and development-related areas be integrated behind one point of accountability.

Companies should acknowledge that measuring talent and applying talent assessment and measurement instruments and tools is complex by nature. Having mentioned in the preceding sections of this chapter which critical attributes need to be considered, the next step is to select fit-for-purpose and well-researched instruments and tools. Whilst the purpose of this chapter is not to provide information about or suggest the instruments and tools to be used, the following is worth noting:

- Companies need to have access to independent expertise.

- Companies that employ such expertise must ensure that the individual is appropriately positioned in the company to have influence over the assessment and measurement strategy.

- Assessment instruments and tools need to be fit for purpose and application must be equitable and fair.

- Reliability and validity studies must be available, and even more so those studies conducted independently of test publishers and vendors.

- Sufficient attention must be given to implementation aspects and how assessment information is used to inform people decisions such as recruitment, development and promotion.

We are arguing that a well-structured leadership talent management process (figure 6.4), implemented and followed by the organisation, can facilitate leadership transitions more effectively.

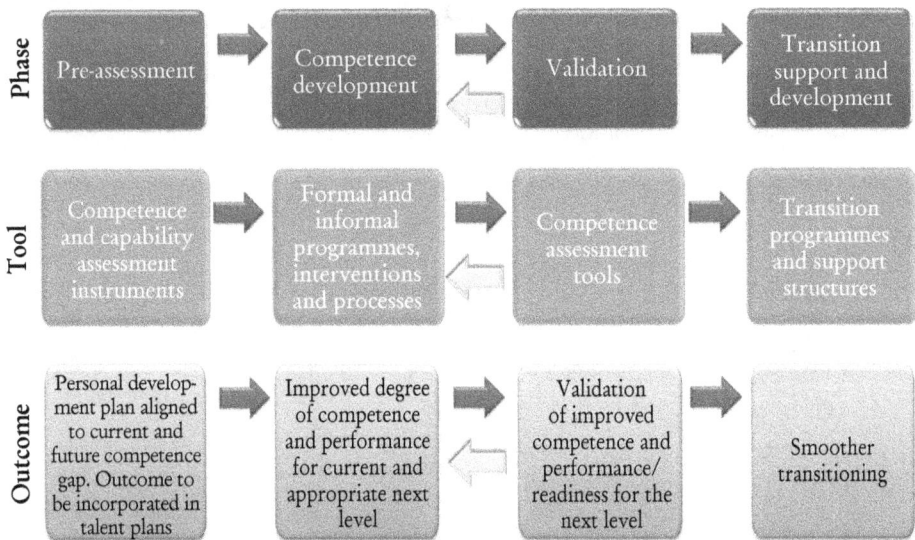

Figure 6.4 Leadership transition process

In the following sections, the leadership transition process is discussed in more detail.

Pre-assessment phase

When identifying talent on which to conduct leadership assessment, the following should be considered:

- An individual's aspiration to advance through the leadership pipeline to more complex roles is not an indication of potential.

- Past performance is not a predictor of potential to succeed in a more complex role.

- 27 per cent of high-potential and talented individuals are at risk of career derailment.[187]

The purpose of this phase is to:

- Confirm potential and ability to perform in a role of increased complexity.

- Assess readiness for transition.

- Identify personal development areas against current-level profile and requirements.[188]

- Identify personal development areas against next-level profile and requirements.

- Allow individuals to identify their own development areas against current and next-level profile and requirements.

- Compile a personal development plan and process informed by potential development areas and individual learning styles.

- Identify organisational trends with regards to development areas for each particular level.

Competence development phase

The purpose of this phase is to:

- Address and develop identified personal development and personal strengths areas as effectively as possible.

- Develop individuals in line with current/next-level profiles and requirements.

- Develop individuals to become fully competent at their current level and performance-ready at the next level.

- Ensure focused development of individuals/groups.

- Align individual development within levels across the organisation.

Validation

The purpose of the validation phase is to:

- Assess individual learning and development as per the personal development plan.

- Validate transition and performance readiness.

- Identify the transition support required.

- Provide input for transition support planning.

- Take stock of process effectiveness.

- Provide input into succession planning or talent review committees.

Transition support

In the transition support phase:

- Individuals are assisted in overcoming the inherent challenges associated with their transitioning to a new role at a more complex level.

- Individuals are assisted to reach the required performance output and value contribution associated with the new role.

This phase needs to integrate with other talent management processes such as performance conversations and career and succession planning. It is also suggested that coaching be utilised to support the individual with his or her transitioning from one level to the next. The line manager plays an instrumental role in the development of the leader.

> **Interesting reading on complexity and talent**
> Tom Foster's Blog: http://managementblog.org/

Conclusion

It is clear that finding and nurturing talent matching the requirements of an ideal competency profile is no longer a viable option in the context of a complex, ever-changing business environment and turbulent economic conditions. The new question to ask is not whether the company's employees and leaders have the right skills; it's whether they have the potential to learn new ones. Organisations should realise that self-aware and agile leaders who have the capability to generate and work with increasing complexity are more relevant for ensuring business performance and organisational success in the future.

Well-designed and integrated talent management and development will produce extraordinary results for the individual as well as the organisation. The learning process should be collaborative in nature, with a philosophy that is supported by reflection, coaching and mentoring as well as action learning.

Chapter 7

New leadership development approaches

Letitia van der Merwe

❄

"We need leaders and not just political leaders. We need leaders in every field, in every institution, in all kinds of situations. We need to be educating our young people to be leaders. And unfortunately, that's fallen out of fashion."
– American historian David McCullough

"I have known talented people who procrastinate indefinitely rather than risk failure." **– Charles Stanley**

In a 2012 survey by the National Leadership Index (NLI), released by the Center for Public Leadership at Harvard Kennedy School and Merriman River Group,[189] 77 per cent of respondents said the United States of America now has a leadership crisis and confidence levels have fallen to the lowest levels in recent times. Literature, and our engagement with clients, indicate that there is significant debate around the impact and effectiveness of leadership development. Some of the research indicates that there is dissatisfaction with the results of leadership development, and questions are also being asked about the way we develop leaders.

There are a number of reasons for this. In our view, one of the key reasons is that we have become so fixated on qualifications and credits that we fail to consider the entire leadership development landscape. We no longer think systemically about leadership development.

We may evoke a bit of controversy here; but we think we find ourselves in the middle of a learning and development system geared towards organisations functioning on business models more appropriate to the 1970s and 1980s. We haven't considered the implications for organisation for the twenty-first century and that people and business leaders need to deal on a daily basis with complexities unheard of and unknown in the past.

Leadership development should form part of an integrated view of leadership. An approach to an integrated model of organisational leadership is reflected in figure 7.1:

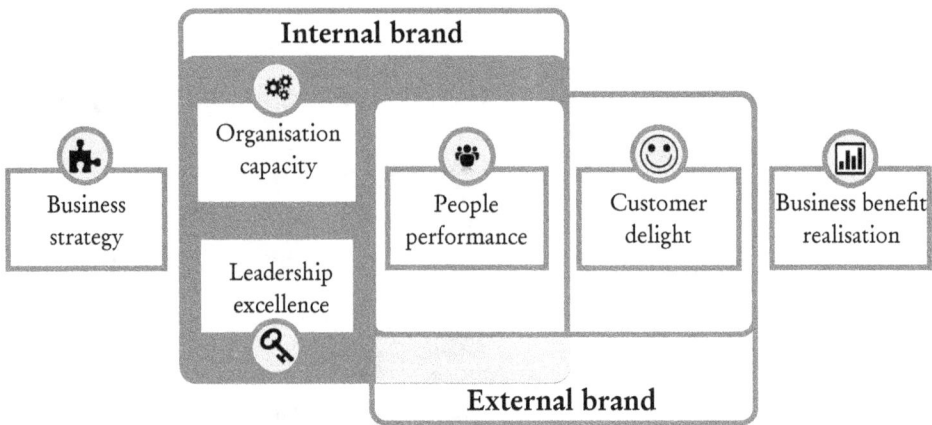

Figure 7.1 Business value model™⁹⁰

In essence, this model suggests that:

1. **Leadership excellence** is in the first instance about the creation of the required **organisational capacity** (people, process and technology) to a) meet the **requirements of all external stakeholders** and b) to ensure **current and future fit to its competitive landscape**.

2. Leadership excellence is then simultaneously the driver of the **internal brand** (or culture), which is determined by the degree to which a) the leadership brand is able to meet the **expectations of employees** so that b) high levels of **employee engagement** (commitment) are achieved.

3. Employee engagement drives **stakeholder delight** or satisfaction.

4. Stakeholder delight or satisfaction leads to **business performance,** which serves as an input to both external stakeholder perceptions and competitive positioning and in this manner creates the **external brand.**

5. It is of key importance that a deliberate process of **strategic communication** be implemented to ensure alignment between the internal leadership brand and the external organisational brand.

Given figure 7.1, what do we know about the current scenario within which leaders have to operate?

Current scenario

It is a lot more volatile, ambiguous and complex than before because of

- changing stakeholder expectations
- organisational capacity, a function of the ability to position within a network of networks
- strategic fit and competitive positioning becoming more time-pressured and fleeting
- global shortage of the requisite leadership talent
- socio-economic and political trends that increasingly lead to mistrust of leadership

The leadership challenge

Given these trends, we need to rethink how we:

- Define leadership beyond the "leader".
- Create a leadership brand that has "bankable" value.
- Create congruence between internal and external perceptions.

This interconnected, complex and volatile environment creates different challenges for leaders as well as different expectations of them. It requires the ability to lead across cultures, time and space. It is becoming increasingly difficult to rely on past experience and it requires that leaders exercise their own judgment more and more.

Leaders are required to understand the organisation as a whole and realise that a change in one area of the system will have an immediate effect on the rest of the system. They need to understand that there is no one "best way" to organise; this depends on the nature of the environment to which the organisation relates. They also need to view their organisations as part of a "network-of-networks", further increasing the complexity to be dealt with. We often refer to this as "and" thinking versus "or" thinking.

This complex environment increasingly requires leaders to be comfortable with ambiguity and a significant difference in the current paradigms and mental models. This requires competencies like systemic thinking, learning agility and wisdom – a concept we define as knowing what to do when you can't draw on past experience.

Impact on leadership development

> The overriding theme of what I've been hearing from clients recently is that they're a bit stunned – shocked, actually – at how the leadership development programs they'd had in place were not able to meet the needs of their business as we've gone through these tremendously disruptive economic changes over the past few years – Bill Pelster, a principal and talent-development leader at New York-based Deloitte LLP.

In our own interaction with clients we hear similar arguments. It's as if organisations assume that if we show leaders what to do they will automatically do it. We have also found that leadership development programmes still follow the typical "MBA development" route, which assumes that teaching leaders mostly business and strategic competencies will result in an increase in their effectiveness. From a leadership development perspective we need to reconsider the way we develop leaders. A more complex environment requires the learning environment to simulate the same level of complexity – a linear cause-and-effect process will just no longer work. Table 7.1 summarises the characteristics of the current versus the more volatile emerging environment leaders have to operate within.

Table 7.1 Current vs emerging environments

Shifting from	To
leader development	leadership capacity-building
leader competence	leadership brand behaviour
ROI of learning and development	benefit realisation of leadership excellence
informal development	integrated development
long-term investment	short- and long-term investment

The business case: why is it important?

Our own research, which has been confirmed by other similar research conducted, shows that the quality of an organisation's leadership community has a direct impact on the level of employee engagement and actual financial results. The quality of the leadership community correlates directly with the capability and competence of leaders – and competence is built through leadership development.

There is likely to be broad agreement that the strategic context within which business operates has seen some dramatic changes. A typical Porter approach[191] suggests that there are significant shifts in the political, economic, social and technological dimensions of our environment. It is our contention that at a fundamental level these changes increase the level of complexity that leaders have to deal with, not only from a long-term perspective, but also in terms of shorter-term actions and processes. One of the consequences of this increased complexity is that organisations need to move beyond the view that individual leaders drive business performance to a perspective that leadership brand linked to the firm or enterprise brand has become critical.

Given the global shortage of leadership talent and talent in general, it is also critically important that organisations translate the leadership brand into organisation-wide leadership capacity. Clearly, as with all other strategic imperatives, it is also important that the organisation takes a perspective on the impact of the leadership capacity-building processes on a broad range of business performance expectations and metrics.

The IBM CEO Study (2010)[192] is a survey of more than 1 500 CEOs from 60 countries and 33 industries worldwide. Some of the key findings are:

- Eight in ten CEOs expect their environment to grow significantly more complex, but only **49 per cent believe their organisations are equipped to deal with it successfully** – the largest leadership challenge identified in eight years of research.

- **More than 60 per cent of CEOs said that industry transformation is the top factor contributing to uncertainty,** indicating a need to discover more innovative ways of managing an organisation's structure, finances, people and strategy.

This raises the question: what is making this world more complex and interconnected and what do we mean by "complexity"? Complexity is defined as that zone between stability and predictability on one hand, and chaos and unpredictability on the other. What is happening is that the rate of chaos and unpredictability is increasing. Organisations are literally becoming more complex to manage due to the large number of interacting elements. The growing complexities of interorganisational relationships between companies and their stakeholders are challenging companies to find new and different ways to manage across once impermeable corporate boundaries. Information inside organisations is ambiguous and many leaders suffer from information overload.

Leadership development best practice

In attempting to compile some form of "list" of best practices in the field of leadership development, we scanned literature produced in the last five years by companies and institutions such as the Corporate Leadership Council, Taleo Corporation, DDI and Deloitte that have a reputation for being among the top thinkers and providers in the domain of leadership development. From these documents, we compiled a list of what these institutions collectively view as the best practices for leadership development (table 7.2).

Table 7.2 Leadership development best practice as seen by companies

Leadership development as business imperative	Research demonstrates that organisations with the highest-quality leaders were 13 times more likely to outperform their competition in key bottom-line metrics such as financial performance, quality of products and services, employee engagement and customer satisfaction.
Aligned to business strategy	All experts in the field of leadership development make this point. The issue of course is to ensure that all leadership processes have the purpose of supporting business strategy.
Executive sponsorship	Logically, if leadership development is part of the business strategy, it should receive as much support and involvement by executives as other business strategies would. It is also true that executive engagement has the biggest impact on the effectiveness of a leadership development programme.
Company-specific leadership competencies	Although there are numerous "models" of leadership behaviour, the research suggests that best practice is for the company to make these specific to their own context. Again, this makes perfect sense if leadership development is supposed to support business strategy. Research also highlights the following five competencies as key to future leadership: • driving and managing change • identifying and developing future talent • fostering creativity and innovation • coaching and developing others • executing organisational strategy
Leadership development curriculum	The research is again almost unanimous in its recommendations that best practice dictates the use of multiple learning methods. The need for experiential learning processes is also specifically highlighted as being of significant value. Organisations with more effective leadership development programmes tend to use four methods more often and more effectively: formal workshops and three types of coaching – manager, internal and external. More effective organisations use a greater number of development methods than the less-effective organisations. However, it's not just the sheer number of methods used that matters, but how those methods are blended together.
Leadership development content	The content of leadership development programmes must build the competencies that are relevant to the company's success. Case studies, projects and conversations should focus on company-specific examples, such as business issues and core processes. The programme should use a common "business language" and instil key messages about the company.

Leadership development as process	Two issues are raised in this aspect, namely 1) leadership development takes time to deliver full value and 2) leadership development should focus on leadership at all levels. This also means that a longer-term perspective must be taken on providing resources for such processes.
Integration with talent management	Another point made in most of the research is that leadership development should be integrated with other talent management strategies and processes. Specific mention is made of succession planning.
Opportunity for personal growth	Leadership development should also be specific to the needs of the individual leader, and in this context processes such as coaching/ mentoring, assessment and feedback are also important. Emphasis is also now placed on identifying and mitigating leadership derailers.
Impact on behaviour	Two key points are made in the research, namely 1) the need to hold leaders accountable for actual behavioural change and 2) the need for the process of leadership development to allow for personal reflection.

In our own experience, the one best practice that stands out in terms of its practical value for clients is the idea of having a set of company-specific leadership competencies. Particularly if there is an inclusive and collaborative process of defining these, the conversations leading to such a model are in and of themselves a deeply meaningful leadership development process. Where HR or a consulting firm defines them as a back-office exercise, in our view they are of limited value.

The second key principle, in our view and experience, is the willingness to accept that building leadership excellence and capacity is not a short-term activity or "programme" but a carefully crafted development process that contains multiple interventions and methodologies. This does not mean that the process needs to become more expensive, and in fact carefully and deliberately crafted processes are often less costly.

The third key principle is that development is only part of the equation to ensure leadership excellence. All of the development in the world will not compensate for poor hiring and promotion decisions.

Emerging trends

"To expand leadership capacity, organisations must not only develop the leadership capacities of individuals but also develop the leadership capacity of collectives" – Ellen van Velsor & Cynthia McCauley

This anecdote from John Mattox[193] really describes so well what we mean by emerging leadership development trends.

Imagine for a moment that you are a sailor on an 18th-century man-of-war, the most powerful sea-going vessel in the British Empire's armada. The brisk ocean breeze is stretching canvas until it's as hard as clam shells and 600 other sailors are racing around the ship performing their duties. This floating city is an amazing system of modern (at that time) technology, well-defined processes, and a strong command-and-control culture. It is a powerful military tool that only is effective when all of the jobs on board are done well.

You are the powder monkey. Two weeks ago when you were kidnapped and pressed into service, you had no intention of joining the royal navy, nor did you know what a powder monkey does. Today, you are able to shuttle packages of black powder from the magazine to any of the 20 cannons on your deck in less than 30 seconds. You learn by following orders barked by a lieutenant. You watch others, model their behavior, and hope that you get it right because you have a strong desire not to be punished by flogging.

Flash forward to 1955 and imagine you are a seaman on a cruiser stationed out of San Diego. You are in a classroom with 29 other recruits listening to a fire control technician explain how to align the sights on a large-calibre machine gun. Once at sea you will be responsible for aiming and firing this weapon to protect your cruiser from incoming enemy aircraft.

The three days of lectures are tedious, but by the fourth day when you get to stand behind the gun, align it, and begin your test-firing drill, you are ready. You watch others practice and take note of how you might do it better. When you step behind it, settle in, and begin firing, you are shocked that the gun kicks harder than a mule. But you lean in with confidence. You know every inch of it, and you are ready to defend the ship. As you step away from the gun, the fire control technician gives you the highest praise he's given to anyone that morning: "Not bad. You missed the target, but you didn't kill anyone. Next!"

Flash forward again to a modern aircraft carrier, the USS Ronald Reagan. You are responsible for maintaining a safe perimeter around the ship using ship-to-air missiles against incoming enemy aircraft.

You are prepared for this role because you studied electrical engineering and software design at the U.S. Naval Academy. You have logged hundreds of hours on computer-based simulators. All the systems manuals are available on the naval intranet, and you are connected to a community of similar operators aboard other ships. Electronic job aids are at your fingertips and protocol checklists are available online in the event of an attack.

It is becoming clearer that the new leadership paradigm differs markedly from what was traditionally viewed as leadership or management. The traditional approach stated that to be effective, management should be founded upon a well-defined hierarchy of authority. Discipline was determined by "management" and interpersonal relationships were encouraged to be impersonal. The emphasis was placed on the "fit" between the environmental challenges and the ability of the individual heroic leader to save the organisation from these challenges.

We know that the days of the individual heroic leader who could inspire organisations are numbered. We know that the demanding complex business world now requires leadership that is able to create shared possible futures – realising a shared, specific chosen future with, through and for people. The future forms the context from which leadership derives justification and meaning on why and how to act.

Leadership is more and more seen as a social process that engages everyone in the community; but organisations have traditionally focused on developing individuals so that they can become better leaders – hence the development of the concept leader. We even refer to individual development plans, putting the emphasis on individual learning.

It clearly does not make sense to focus only on developing individual leaders, and there seems to be growing recognition that the emphasis should be on developing leadership as a collective. What we are envisaging is that the future will very likely be about developing leadership communities and networks of leaders. Knowing which skills leaders need to develop is only half the battle. There are many ways leaders can develop, and a variety of tools they can use to enhance their learning experience. The process of learning is usually formal, structured and directed. But in real day-to-day operations, leaders are learning all the time, outside classrooms and on the job.

What might developing a leadership community look like?

In chapter 3 we defined leadership community as the nature, dynamics and evolution of a leadership grouping. The leadership group of an organisation forms a community of practice with its own ideology, brand, beliefs, value set and code of practice. Associated with the leadership community is a certain leadership culture and climate: the interpersonal, team and organisation-wide dynamics between and amongst the organisation's leadership.

The quality of the leadership community of an organisation forms the leadership capital of the organisation. It thus critical that the make-up, dynamics and evolution of leadership communities are clearly understood and managed. This will be reflected in the organisation's leadership brand. Developing leadership community is about developing leadership at all levels of the organisation – it's not about only considering the needs of a few or of the individual. This also implies that the responsibility for development moves away from the organisation to the individual.

We think that some of the following factors should also be present in an organisation where people take greater ownership of their development:

- recognition that in complex environments, business strategies cannot be executed without leadership excellence

- recognition that new methods for development need to be used and that traditional horizontal development won't be enough

- leaders to be educated on research into how development occurs, why it works better when they own it and what the benefits are for them

- utilisation of new technologies, such as those which allow people to take control of their own feedback and gather ongoing suggestions for improvement

- creation of a culture in which it is safe to take the type of risk required to conduct work into the discomfort zone

In terms of new ways of doing leadership development, we are also starting to see some of the following key leadership development trends emerging more and more. They are usually divided into three categories: formal, nonformal and informal learning. What is informal learning? According to Michael Hanley's blog,[194] e-learning curve, formal, informal and nonformal learning are defined in the following way:

- Formal learning: learning objectives are set by the training department, which also provides the learning product. Formal learning often leads to certification.

- Informal learning: the learner sets the goals and objectives. Learning is not necessarily structured in terms of time and effort; it is often incidental and unlikely to lead to certification.

- Nonformal learning: someone in the organisation who is not part of the learning department (for example, a line manager, supervisor or business leader) sets a learning objective or task. Learning does not lead to certification.

> KnowledgeJump offers a useful tool called the Periodic Table of Learning Elements (www.knowledgejump.com/agile/periodic.html), which provides insight into various components of formal and informal learning.

Social learning

Social learning solutions can strongly support formal learning structures by accelerating change and innovation and building a knowledge-sharing culture within an organisation. This does not mean Twitter-like status updates or dumping content on a learning portal. Social learning is not social media, and using social media doesn't make learning "social". Social learning is the way most of us learn most things; for example we learned to talk through interaction with others.

Social learning is not and should not be about the tools. Many a learning and development practitioner has told us that they have set up the community but no one uses it, or they update the blogs but no one reads them.

It's probably because we often think of social learning as providing tools and processes and do not always consider how human beings learn socially. When social learning happens, people often express it as "solving a problem". It becomes part of the way they go about work. Social learning should allow people to make their own connections and to make contextual meaning based on their current and desired future activities, rather than an end point defined by someone else within the organisation.

Gamification

Another trend linked to social learning is the whole concept of gamification. Though the term "gamification" was coined in 2002 by Nick Pelling, a British-born computer programmer and inventor, it did not gain popularity until 2010. The concept is usually defined as the use of game thinking and game mechanics in nongame contexts to engage users in solving problems and increase users' own contributions. From a leadership development perspective, two examples in particular have emerged that show how gamification platforms are being leveraged to develop future leaders. At the systems integration company NTT DATA and the well-known consulting company Deloitte, gamification is being used successfully. Both NTT DATA and Deloitte claim that what is making this so successful is the ability to use game mechanics to drive greater levels of engagement and employee motivation. According to both companies, gamification should not be just about fun – it should be consistent with an organisation's analytics-driven approach to workforce management and aligned to their business goals.

There is enormous hype about gamification at the moment; however, we are not sure if this hype will last. It may create a reinforcement of the concept "edutainment" – I only learn when I'm entertained, and therefore I constantly start looking for the next big thing. Having said this, what is great about the gamification movement is the willingness to try something new and that they understand the importance of learner motivation and experience. We believe that the principles can be very usefully applied in more self-directed learning applications.

More emphasis on leadership transition support and development

Typical leadership transitions include:

- moving from one organisational level to next, for example senior management to executive management

- moving from function to the next, for example manufacturing to research and development

- moving from one contextual complexity level to next, for example, a local, single product/client organisation to a global, diversified organisation

- moving from one organisational role to the next, for example delivery to support

As discussed in the previous chapter, we know that leader transitions are "high-risk" points with significant cost implications (not only financial) to the organisation. A survey of over 200 company CEOs and presidents yielded an estimate of 6.2 months for the typical new leader to reach break-even point – the point at which they are net creators of value for their organisations.[195] Leadership transitions have an impact not only on the individual leader, but also on the "transition network" and the organisation. Smoother transitions will result in better performance in less time. We are of the view that in the future more emphasis will be placed on equipping leaders to make transitions more smoothly.

More emphasis on innovation in leadership development methods

There is clearly a call for a more innovative approach to leadership development. Research conducted by Mannaz[196] highlights the following ideas that are likely to shape the future of leadership development initiatives in the next few years:

- working more with other organisations (in a consortium, organising joint leadership development seminars, looking for cross-pollination of development with others organisations, etc)

- creating a learning culture (asking people to take responsibility for their own learning process and development, stressing life-long learning, encouraging self-directed learning (reading/viewing/listening) etc)

- including customers and suppliers in leadership development initiatives (involving complete teams in workshops with customers and suppliers, using customer surveys to open a dialogue, etc)

- promoting group-oriented development in intact teams (team processes where the leader facilitates the process, training as they lead)

- involving the board (executives as role models, showing required changes, showing commitment, using web 2.0 technology, podcasts etc)

- improving mobility (short-term assignments, encouraging more mobility between functions and business areas, ensuring leaders are exposed to a variety of challenges and aspects of the organisation as a development challenge and opportunity)

- more emphasis on senior leaders coaching, mentoring, teaching and facilitating (training leaders to teach, train and facilitate, inviting them to do it with their own team)

- cross-cultural awareness and understanding (developing a higher awareness of cultures and functional cultures using workshops, assignments, projects etc);

- nonclassical learning journeys (eg meeting and learning from nonprofit organisations etc)

- exploring second life (inviting retired executives, leaders or professionals to share their experience and expertise)

- looking at development within the entire value chain (ecosystem, sustainability)

More emphasis on taking personal accountability for leadership development

In most organisations the predominant paradigm seems to be that "The company must develop me". While there might be some merit to this view, it is equally important that leaders also take responsibility for their own growth. Good development practices tell us that people's motivation to grow is at its highest when they feel a sense of ownership of their own development journey.

At the moment leadership development still very much involves 1) a professional who manages learning and 2) a learner (leader) who implements the learning. We think the future could be one in which leaders will manage the learning and the learning and development professional will support the process and the leadership community.

There are three levels of specific behavioural change required in moving towards a model of greater development ownership for the individual: the individual level, the interpersonal level and the group or organisational level. First, individuals must be willing to change their own thinking and feelings about development. Second, people need to become skilful at making contracts with one another and holding one another accountable for development results. Third, the leadership community needs to promote responsible and constructive conversations by developing norms for directing development between individuals. These behavioural changes can help create a constructive learning culture of shared ownership.

Summary

We are entering a new era of leadership development. It is likely that the transformation of leadership development will start with those brave enough to challenge the status quo and build small pockets of innovation and excellence. In the next section we provide you with some guidelines and ideas on how to do this practically, while keeping the integrated picture in mind.

Leadership development: purpose, process and content

This section is called purpose, process and content, because in our experience people responsible for leadership development inside organisations often jump to the content level. We have developed a leadership development conversation framework in which we define excellence as consisting of four building blocks, as outlined in figure 7.2:

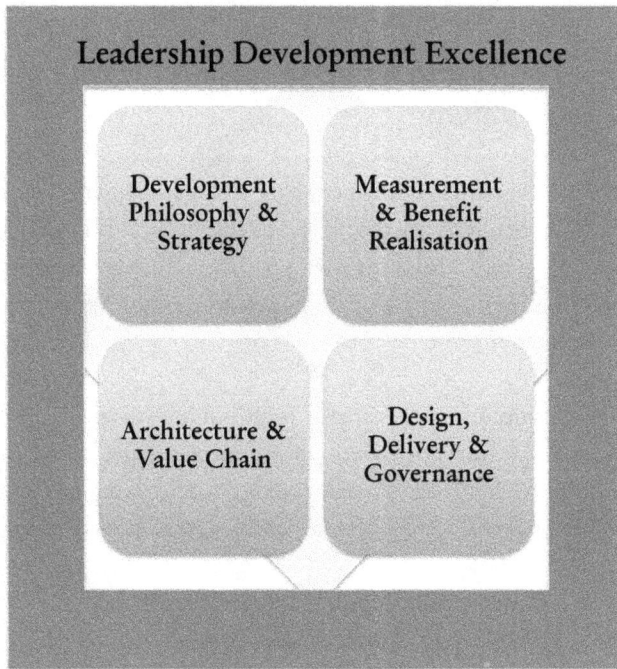

Figure 7.2 Leadership development conversation framework

Development, philosophy and strategy

A learning philosophy reflects what an organisation believes about learning. It answers not the "how" questions (process) nor the "what" questions (of content), but the "why" questions. Why are we learning as an organisation? What role does learning play in our organisational strategy? This approach applies to leadership development as well.

EXAMPLES

- Leadership is a key element of business strategy.

- It should inform and be informed by the human capital strategy and be based on a shared understanding of the organisation's human capital, plus the leadership philosophy and the values it wishes to entrench.

- It should focus on creating a leadership brand that both has external stakeholder value and creates the culture the organisation desires.

- It should focus on developing leadership capacity throughout the organisation – not only individual leadership development.

- It should be integrated by taking into consideration the relationship between leadership development and technical/functional development.

- It should be holistic, taking into consideration both organisational and individual (or personal) development, and creating a shared understanding of the leadership development "roadmap".

The leadership strategy and the learning philosophy inform the leadership development strategy – which specifies the actions that must be taken to retain, develop or acquire the leaders and the leadership skills required by the business strategy and to build the leadership community.

Because the link between business strategy, leadership strategy and leadership development strategy has so often been missed, many organisations do not have either a defined leadership strategy or a leadership development strategy at all. The Corporate Leadership Council supports our thinking in terms of the necessity of a leadership development strategy, and the following extract is taken from their white paper Developing a leadership strategy: a critical ingredient for organizational success.[197]

A cursory examination of organisations without a clear leadership development strategy will reveal that leadership development consists of an assortment of programs that are roughly tied to the level of participants, rather than to a careful assessment of business needs. Competency models, when they have been customized to fit the business, are often generic, backward looking or only loosely tied to the learning activities that take place. Different units or locations in the organization may have their own approaches to development, utilizing different activities, programs and vendors. The end result is a horrendous waste of time and money, as well as missed opportunities to make important contributions to organizational success.

Participants in non-strategic development programs may sense that they are being "put through the mill" and that what's important is "checking the box" rather than applying what they are learning to key organizational objectives. Even if they are able to derive personal insights that they want to put into practice, they will often find that there is no support for them to do so. While shortcuts may appear to save time and money, in the long run they are a poor investment because they don't produce individual or organizational transformation. To achieve lasting and substantial benefits, learning must be applied to real organizational issues. Moreover, learning must take place in the collective, not just on the part of individuals. It's how formal and informal leaders work together that determines whether or not organizations succeed in implementing strategies and adapting to change, not individual leaders acting alone. Leadership development activities must change the context within which leading takes place, not simply the mindsets or capabilities of individual leaders. While capable individuals are the foundation for success, organizations require coordinated action to improve effectiveness or shift directions. Individual development and coaching will only get the organization so far; breakthroughs require attention to leadership cultures and collective leadership capabilities.

Architecture and value chain

Learning architecture translates the learning philosophy and strategy into the physical operating model of the unit within the organisation responsible for learning and development. The architecture also ensures that development and capacity-building are aligned to other processes within the sphere of human capital, for example talent management.

What we are suggesting is that organisations give more mindful application to setting up the learning architecture. This should be informed by the purpose of the learning and development and the actual strategy. Important questions to ask here are:

- What is the purpose of learning and development?
- How will we know we are successful?
- What real business benefit will it add in terms of a systemic view of the individual, the team, the organisation and the bigger community?
- How will it enable us to compete better as an organisation (especially during these tough economic times)?

As stated above, what we don't want to see is leadership development becoming a mechanistic model where people are just pushed through training programmes. In our view an effective architecture (operating model) should be informed by the following design principles (or design criteria):

- clear ownership, responsibilities and accountabilities
- simplicity
- minimisation of duplication
- standardisation, agility/flexibility
- value-add
- tight (ie centralisation) and loose (ie decentralisation)
- direct line of sight between actions and results/outcomes
- involvement/participation
- cost-effectiveness
- responsiveness
- customisation/localisation
- integration/seamlessness

How these principles are applied is a function of the organisational context, purpose and challenges. Some organisations have opted for a model based on the corporate university. In most cases, corporate universities are not universities in the strict sense of the word. The traditional university is an educational institution which grants both undergraduate and postgraduate degrees in a variety of subjects, as well as conducting original scientific research. In contrast, a corporate university typically limits its scope to providing job-specific, indeed company-specific, training for the managerial personnel of the parent corporation. Corporate universities are most commonly found in the United States of America, a nation that has no official legal definition of the term "university".

In South Africa the term "university" is governed by legislation and corporate companies are not allowed to call themselves universities. What is more commonly found is the concept of the leadership development academy.

The leadership development academy/institute

Corporate universities were first created as an enhancement to traditional training departments. This new approach was designed to align the training arm of companies with the organisations' vision and strategy. Probably one of the most famous and most studied corporate universities is General Electric's – GE at Crotonville. Often the leadership development academy/institute forms part of the bigger corporate university, although I once encountered a leadership academy as an extension of an organisation's strategy department. The logic for this was rather simple – strategy and leadership were seen as two sides of the same coin.

At least in my mind, a leadership development academy/institute serves as a metaphor for continuous leadership development. Figure 7.3 demonstrates the steps typically followed to set up such an entity:

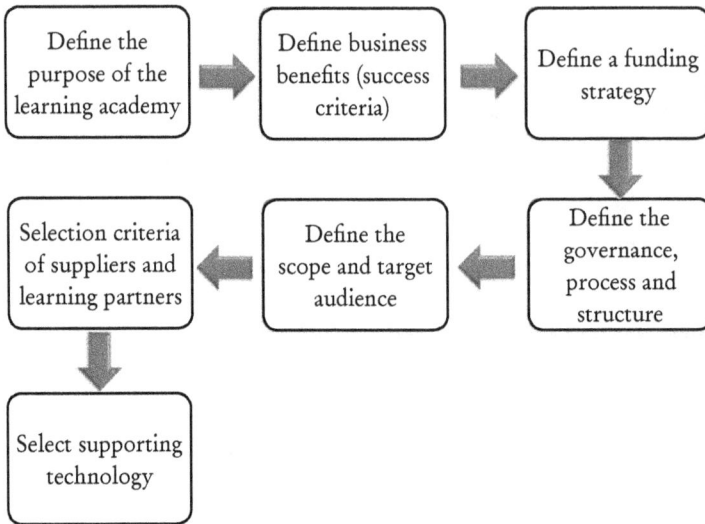

Figure 7.3 Building a leadership development academy/institute

---

EXAMPLES: Eskom Leadership Institute[198]

The Eskom Leadership Institute (ELI) was formed in 2011 to drive implementation of the Eskom Leadership Strategy and ensure its alignment to the overall business strategy with Eskom's Chief Executive, Mr Brian Dames, taking it into his own office to demonstrate his passion and commitment to leadership and executive talent management. The ELI consists of the following areas: Executive, Senior, Middle Management and Supervisory Development, Capability Assessment and Diagnostics and Leadership Strategy and Executive Talent Management.

The underpinning philosophy of ELI is focused on embracing an "inside-out" approach. This approach assists leaders to first get to their underlying beliefs, attitudes and values (mind-set) that perpetuate ineffective behaviour, before moving towards the leadership domains of others, the organisation and the world. The learning process is designed to first obtain awareness of "what is driving my behaviour?" such as "what are my blind spots?" and "what assumptions am I making and why?" in the context of self, others, organisation and world. This consistent inside-out approach is aligned to a specific Eskom leadership brand. This brand serves as the filter through which all leadership programmes, practices, diagnostics and assessments are performed.

Design, delivery and governance

Learning and development solutions, especially in our context, are still very much based on an education model – a model very applicable to teaching but not to workplace learning. Our thinking is still very much classroom-based and doesn't always recognise that people learn without being in a classroom.

Leadership development process

For a long time we have thought about leadership development as working out what competencies a leader should possess and then helping individual managers to develop them. In our own mind the leadership development process should take into account the development level together with a leadership complexity level and the integration across leadership levels. Figure 7.4 shows a conceptual example.

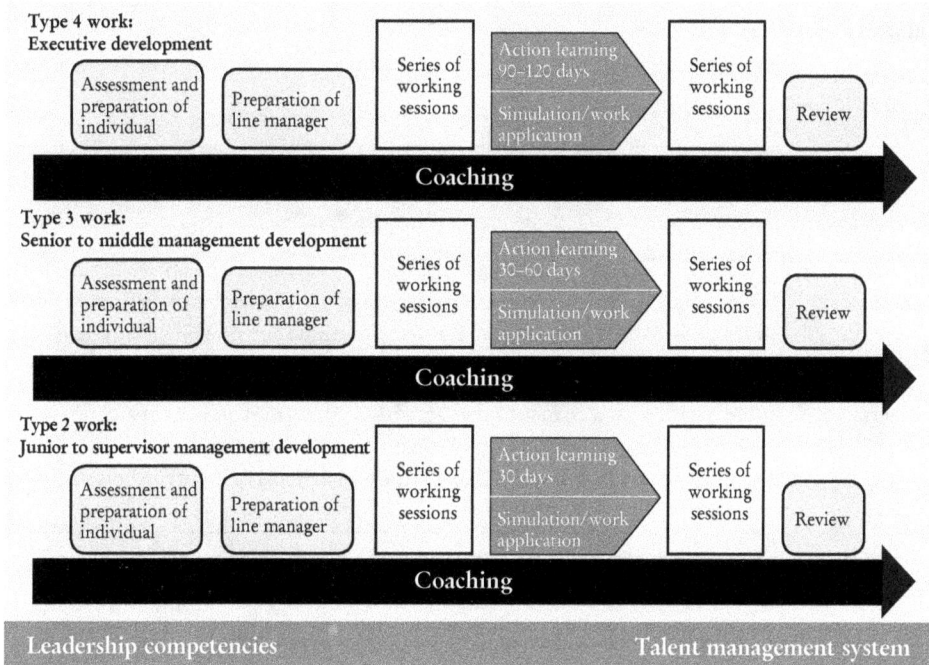

Figure 7.4 Example of the leadership development process

Probably one of the most important aspects of the leadership development process is how senior leaders engage participants in the learning process. Jeff Immelt, GE's chairman and CEO, spends more than one-third of his time on leadership development – setting the tone for leaders at Crotonville and worldwide. The learning process should also cater for developing the leadership community and not only the individual leader.

While many organisations say that they need leaders at all levels of the business, this statement appears inconsistent with their practices as long as they continue to train and develop only their "elite" leaders. The leadership development process is about how to develop leaders across the organisation. In chapter 9 we share a couple of practical examples.

Learning design, delivery and complexity

There is a lot to say for workplace-based learning. However, what we often find is that the people in the workplace need to deal with greater complexities than the learning environment offers.

If one subscribes to the notion of different levels of complexity inside organisations, development processes in organisations should require participants to work on problems that are appropriate to their current level of work complexity. Table 7.2 highlights this thinking.

Table 7.2 Complexity of problem-solving

Type of complexity	Nature of complexity
Quality	Overcome challenges in linear pathway.
Service	Overcome challenges in linear pathway, while at the same time reflecting on experience and things learned so as to diagnose emerging problems and initiate actions to prevent or overcome the problems identified.
Practice	Find a path with a chance of coping with short-term requirements while providing initial stages of a realistic path towards long-term goals of between 12 and 24 months. Change to alternative paths if initial choice is unsatisfactory.
Strategic development	Run several interacting projects, pacing them in relation to one another in resourcing and in time. Make trade-offs between tasks in order to maintain progress along the composite route to the goal.
Strategic intent	Cope with constantly shifting events and consequences with many variables using judgement – sense interconnections between variables in the organisation and environment, constantly adjusting them in relation to each other.

Development can also consider the movement up to a higher level of complexity. Developmental movement from one stage to the next is usually driven by limitations in the current stage. When you are confronted with increased complexity and challenges that can't be reconciled with what you know and can do at your current level, you are pulled to take the next step.[199]

Learning delivery

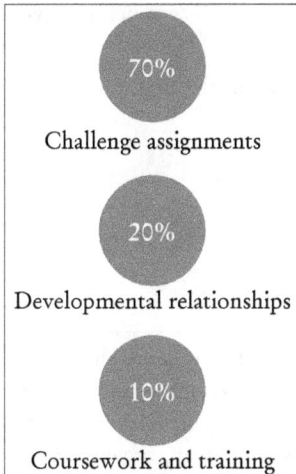

70%

Challenge assignments

20%

Developmental relationships

10%

Coursework and training

Learning delivery refers to the delivery of the blended learning approach. Blended learning is often defined as a mix of classroom and virtual training events. But blended learning for leadership goes beyond coursework – it is about the engagement of leadership with the organisational leadership context. In our mind true blended learning is a combination of formal learning and workplace-based or "informal" learning opportunities – addressing all segments of the 70:20:10 rule. The 70:20:10 rule was pioneered by the Center for Creative Leadership[200] and based on 30 years of study of how executives learn to lead. It rests on the belief that leadership is learned through doing.

Figure 7.5 The 70-20-10 rule for leadership development

Measurement and benefit realisation

The purpose of measuring learning impact broadly has two points of departure. On the one hand there is the approach that attempts to determine to what degree development processes and programmes have some demonstrable "value". The typical and well-known approaches of Kirkpatrick and Philips are examples of this approach; they both at some point in their models move to the second approach, which is to shift the focus away from development per se towards the actual business benefits realised.

A key consideration in rethinking how we design and deliver learning solutions is making participants aware when learning has actually occurred – especially with the currently predominant mindset that learning only happens "if I receive credits towards a qualification".

From the above we can see that the new and emerging approaches in learning and development focus predominantly in what is traditionally known as informal development. While this in no way suggests that informal development is necessarily unplanned, learning will happen outside the "control" of the "training department". Some new developments in this area are looking at ways of collecting or recording learning experiences that matter. Reflective practices are good tools for individual realisation of learning that has occurred, but don't necessarily apply to learning that has happened within natural intact teams or even across teams.

Reflective practices also do not necessarily help the organisation to keep records of learning that is shareable, trackable and quantifiable. In our opinion we need to rethink how we view the measurement of learning and development from different perspectives.

Measurement and benefit realisation are discussed in more detail in the next chapter.

Summary

According to McKinsey Quarterly 2014,[201] leadership development programmes fail for the following reasons:

Overlooking context	Context is a critical component of successful leadership. Too many training initiatives we come across rest on the assumption that one size fits all and that the same group of skills or style of leadership is appropriate regardless of strategy, organisational culture or CEO mandate.
Decoupling reflection from real work	Tie leadership development to real on-the-job projects that have a business impact and improve learning. The ability to push training participants to reflect, while also giving them real work experiences to apply new approaches and hone their skills, is a valuable combination in emerging markets.
Underestimating mind-sets	Becoming a more effective leader often requires changing behaviour. But although most companies recognise that this also means adjusting underlying mind-sets, too often these organisations are reluctant to address the root causes of why leaders act the way they do. Doing so can be uncomfortable for participants.
Failing to measure results	We frequently find that companies pay lip service to the importance of developing leadership skills but have no evidence to quantify the value of their investment. When businesses fail to track and measure changes in leadership performance over time, they increase the odds that improvement initiatives won't be taken seriously.

We hope that what we have accomplished in this chapter is to help you to understand that leadership development is not about clustering loose leadership development programmes. It starts with a leadership development strategy that clearly defines the leadership development process and the leadership development content.

In the next chapter we look at measurement.

Chapter 8

Not all that is measured counts

Anton Verwey and Letitia van der Merwe
Contributing author: Yolandi Havemann

❄

"Not everything that can be counted *counts*, and *not everything* that *counts* can be counted. **– Albert Einstein**

"If a measurement matters at all, it is because it must have some conceivable effect on decisions and behaviour. If we can't identify a decision that could be affected by a proposed measurement and how it could change those decisions, then the measurement simply has no value." **– Douglas W Hubbard**

In one of our client companies we fondly refer to their rigorous measurement practices as "If it moves they measure it, and if it doesn't move they will kick it until it moves." This is said with good humour but it doesn't take away today's modern organisations' relentless desire to measure business value. Earnings, sales forecasts and risk and compliance measures are the order of the day, but despite acknowledging the importance of leadership as a value driver, few companies deliberately measure whether they have "enough leaders" and the "right leaders" to run their businesses, both today and in the future. In a recent study conducted by Deloitte in 2015,[202] building leadership capacity remains a top CEO-level priority, yet the data suggests that companies have made little or no progress in closing the capability gap.

Gandossy and Guarnieri (2008)[203] observed more and more companies investing in leadership programmes, but for many, the right measures and metrics of whether or not those programmes are contributing towards building the required leadership capacity still remain obscure. All too many companies are flying blind, with little or no insight into what really matters – and what doesn't – in identifying and developing leaders.

Can you answer the following questions in terms of your own organisation?

- To what degree is there clarity and alignment on our desired leadership brand?

- To what degree is there clarity and alignment on our required leadership capacity for now and the future to meet business/strategic needs?

- To what degree do our development processes link to business requirements?

- To what degree do our development processes lead to sustained and observable behaviour change?

- To what degree do our leadership development processes lead to higher levels of employee engagement/commitment?

- To what degree can we see improvement in business results such as productivity, customer satisfaction, profitability (or other measures related to our strategy)?

If you don't have answers to these questions, hopefully this chapter can give you at least a starting point for measuring leadership capacity and leadership impact within your own organisation.

Why we measure leadership capacity and impact

Simply, it seems to us that the purpose of measuring leadership impact broadly has two points of departure. On the one hand there is the approach that attempts to determine to what degree leadership development processes and programmes have some demonstrable "value". The typical and well-known approaches of Kirkpatrick and Philips are examples of this approach. At some point in their models, both move to the second approach, which is to shift the focus away from development per se and towards the actual improvement in value added by leadership, or business benefits realised. The following are the salient points of these two approaches:

The Kirkpatrick four-level model typically measures:

- *reaction of students* – what they thought and felt about the training

- *learning* – the resulting increase in knowledge or capability

- *behaviour* – extent of behaviour and capability improvement and implementation/ application

- *results* – the effects on the business or environment resulting from the trainee's performance

The Phillips model measures similar constructs, namely

- participant reaction to and satisfaction with the training programme and participants' plans for action
- learning: skills and knowledge gains
- application and implementation: changes in on-the-job application, behaviour change and implementation
- business impact
- Return on Investment (ROI): compares the monetary value of the business outcomes with the costs of the training programme

This is illustrated in figure 8.1.

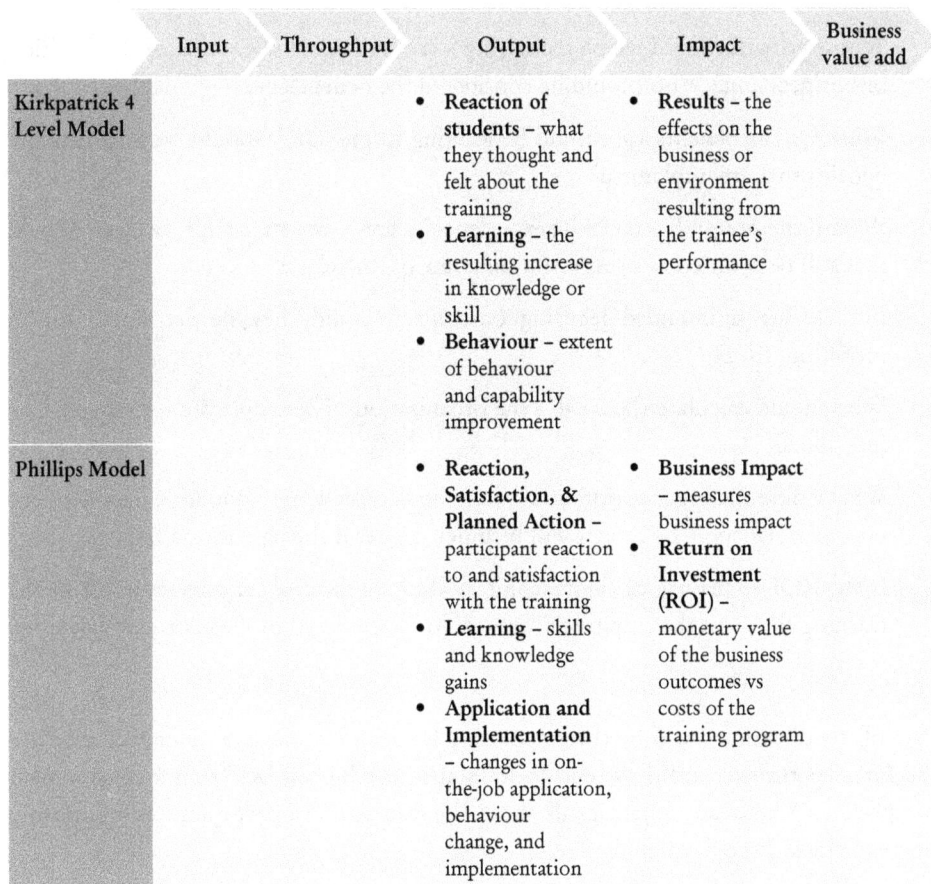

	Input	Throughput	Output	Impact	Business value add
Kirkpatrick 4 Level Model			• **Reaction of students** – what they thought and felt about the training • **Learning** – the resulting increase in knowledge or skill • **Behaviour** – extent of behaviour and capability improvement	• **Results** – the effects on the business or environment resulting from the trainee's performance	
Phillips Model			• **Reaction, Satisfaction, & Planned Action** – participant reaction to and satisfaction with the training • **Learning** – skills and knowledge gains • **Application and Implementation** – changes in on-the-job application, behaviour change, and implementation	• **Business Impact** – measures business impact • **Return on Investment (ROI)** – monetary value of the business outcomes vs costs of the training program	

Figure 8.1 Learning measurement models

It seems to us that the inherent assumptions of both approaches can be summarised as follows:

- It measures **training** impact.

- The unit of measure remains **individual** skill.

- It assumes a direct relationship between skills acquired and job/organisation impact.

Whilst there may be some broad consensus on how the "value" of leadership development may be calculated, there is significantly less clarity and consensus on how the business benefit of leadership itself may be determined. The reason for this lack of clarity is that the answer depends on what question we are asking, and of whom. The following examples illustrate the point:

- Whose growth should we be measuring – the individual's? Or that of the function or business unit? Who should be considered the beneficiary?

- What are the benefits we should be looking to measure? Should we also measure benefits that are unplanned?

- What if the person has an "Aha experience" a few years after taking a class? Would that still be counted as a successful outcome of that class?

- If there are unintended learning outcomes, should they be accounted for in measuring ROI?

- Who should calculate the ROI – the organisation? The employee's manager? The individual?

- Who should the organisation invest in – the select few high-potential people or the poor performers? The return will be much higher if the base is smaller.

- Is the ROI a measure of the teaching skill of the facilitator, or does it reflect the learning ability of the employee? Or should the credit go to the instructional design team?

Part of the dilemma could be that measuring leadership value-add or impact is left to the HR department, and they tend to look at leadership impact from a development perspective. What really intrigues us about the leadership impact question is probably best explained through examples.

Johnson & Johnson, which defines itself as an organisation that "believe[s] our first responsibility is to the doctors, nurses and patients, to mothers and fathers and all others who use our products and services," is well known for developing leaders who provide scientifically sound, high-quality products and services that help heal, cure disease and improve quality of life. General Electric, whose motto is "imagination at work", is well known for its internal leadership bench strength and the ability of its leaders to manage other companies successfully. The Disney Institute not only focuses on developing its own leaders, but also offers to share its approach and practices with other organisations.

What do these companies have in common? The most obvious answer is that they go beyond standard-issue leadership development; but in our minds they create true leadership communities by not only focusing on individual leaders, but also building a collective and shared leadership capacity. Their leadership capacity-building goes beyond a traditional ROI approach – they unlock what we have labelled "business benefits".

In our quest to understand how to measure leadership impact we explored both academic and corporate literature for alternative methods that are not found only in the field of learning and development.

Introduction to models and approaches

The literature contains a variety of models positioning leadership impact in slightly different ways. In this section we unpack this in more detail.

Leadership brand as business benefit

Leadership brand was introduced by Ulrich and Smallwood,[204] and their definition is "a reputation for developing exceptional managers with a distinct set of talents that are uniquely geared to fulfil customers' and investors' expectations. A company with a leadership brand inspires faith that employees and managers will consistently make good on the firm's promises."

They explain this by stating that although companies have spent millions on their own corporate universities, most have failed to develop true leadership bench strength. From their perspective, in many cases the approach to leadership training is detached from what the organisation stands for in the eyes of customers and investors. Rather, training is the same from company to company: a senior executive extols the importance of leadership; outside experts talk about business strategy, elicit 360° feedback, or take personality assessments; and leadership practices are piecemeal and seldom integrated with the organisation's brand, let alone with the daily operations of the organisation.

Ulrich and Smallwood support our thinking, as they also believe that at the root of this problem is a persistent focus on developing the individual leader. In our own experience organisations rely on a competency model that identifies a generic set of competencies (and some unfortunately still believe in ideal personality traits) and then try to find and build individual leaders that fit the model. Ulrich and Smallwood summarise their thinking eloquently in stating: "We believe that long-term success – the kind that lasts generation after generation – depends on making the critical distinction between leaders and leadership. A focus on leaders emphasises the personal qualities of the individual; a focus on leadership emphasises the methods that secure the ongoing good of the firm and, in the process, also builds future leaders."

Figure 8.2 positions leadership within the context of corporate leadership branding.

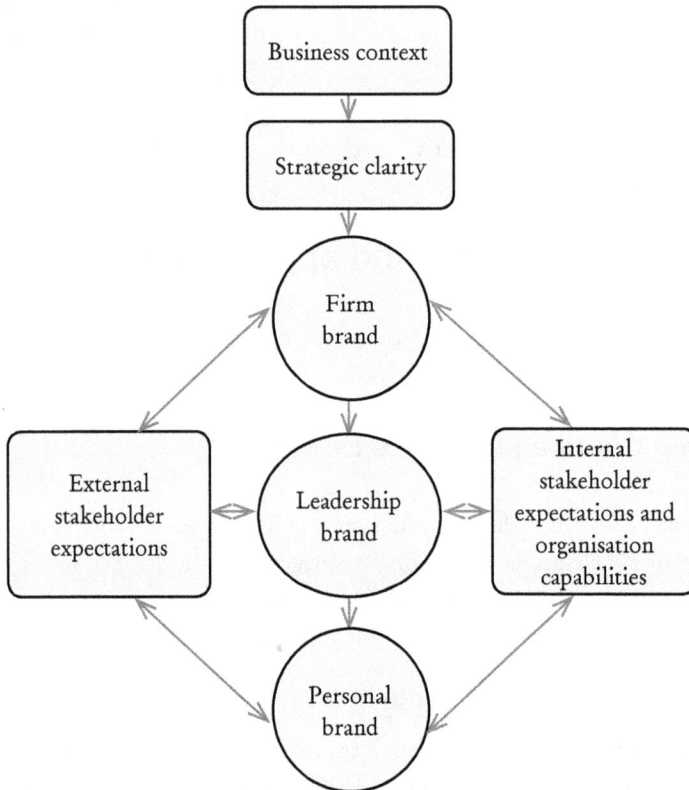

Figure 8.2 Leadership branding[205]

For us this thinking is clear – leadership impact can never be about the individual leader. This model clearly positions leadership at a strategic level, but in addition also implies that to a large extent the ability to build and leverage such a leadership brand also requires alignment of the personal brands of individual leaders to the desired corporate leadership brand.

Modified service profit chain

The service profit chain introduced by Owen and Heskett[206] in a simplistic form establishes relationships between profitability, customer loyalty and employee satisfaction. In their original work, the links in the chain (which they call propositions) are as follows:

- Business results such as profit and growth are stimulated primarily by customer loyalty.

- Customer loyalty is a direct result of customer satisfaction with the value of products and services received.

- Value-adding products and services are created by satisfied, loyal and productive employees.

- Employee satisfaction results primarily from high-quality internal support services and policies that enable employees to deliver value.

In our own thinking, and building on the work of Owen and Heskett, the model in figure 8.3 positions leadership as a critical factor impacting on strategy and employee engagement, and is seen as a driver of both the internal brand, or internal culture, and external experience or external perception of leadership (leadership brand).

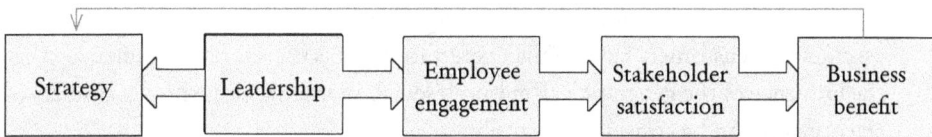

Figure 8.3 Modified service profit chain[207]

We have worked with a number of organisations in a variety of industries, sometimes across the elements in figure 8.3 and sometimes with a focus on specific elements of the figure. A reflection on the relationships and patterns that we discovered and confirmed with these clients is outlined below:

- The quality and continuity of leadership is a key variable in the creation of competitive strategy and a culture that supports in a sustainable manner the execution of that strategy.

- The failure to address culture as a key variable almost inevitably dooms efforts at transformation or improvements to failure.

- Attracting and retaining the appropriate and required talent through a focused employee value proposition will remain a challenge in the future.

- Increasingly, and perhaps because of the global pressures on efficiency and effectiveness, a strategic perspective on organisation and work design is becoming more important than ever.

- Increasingly, and for a variety of reasons, corporate reputation amongst diverse stakeholders is becoming a key competitive lever.

The inherent dilemma with each of these is that they require a long-term perspective from the leaders in organisations. There is no quick fix to address leadership brand or capacity. There is no simple way to improve levels of employee engagement. You simply cannot change customer experience overnight. The analogy we increasingly use with clients is that strategic leadership is more like farming than it is like hunting, and yet we have to be quick and decisive whilst at the same time taking the long view. In our own experience the following are some lessons learnt and some recommendations for organisations that want to explore the measurement of leadership impact.

External context

In the first instance, the external context of the organisation should be understood in specific detail. Some of the issues to be clarified are:

- A single quantitative (questionnaire) measure of customer-experienced value assumes that customers have similar expectations. It is therefore recommended that the influence of the geographical/cultural/social/economic context of customers of the organisation be considered as well.

- Single instruments claiming to be adequate to measure customer value across industries may be so general in nature that they in fact add little value to the understanding of the uniqueness of an industry, the products/services it provides, and the key stakeholders it has to interact with given its own context. Instruments should be customised to reflect the unique dynamics of the industry within which the organisation operates.

- Using industry benchmarks for comparison purposes assumes that all organisations are similar. Organisations should rather use internal benchmarks and baseline data when deciding on actions and initiatives.

Relationship dynamics

The following recommendations can be made about developing insight into the relationships between the various elements.

- Firstly, research of this kind almost by definition has to be longitudinal in nature. It is in all likelihood not so much the employee climate and customer value that are related to one another, but rather changes in employee climate over time that will impact on customer-experienced value over time, which will in turn impact on changes in financial measures over time.

- Secondly, financial measures as the only measures of performance should also be reconsidered. For example, in economic circumstances where all players in an industry are under pressure in terms of revenues and profits, they may still be delivering customer excellence through a positive workforce. In such cases, other measures of performance may be more accurate ways to assess the organisation's long-term sustainability.

- Thirdly, whilst focusing on creating leadership capacity, a focus should also be retained on the internal processes, structures and systems of the organisation as an "enabling environment" to achieve business results through leadership excellence.

- Finally, it is suggested that all research on perceptions of customers, employees and other key stakeholders includes qualitative research to enrich and augment "the message of the numbers".

It is very important that this phase should integrate with other talent management processes such as performance conversations and career and succession planning. We also suggest that coaching be utilised to support the individual in the transition from one level to the next, and that the current line manager play an instrumental role in the development of the leader.

Integrated Leadership Strategy model

The model in figure 8.4 shows an integration of the approaches articulated by institutions such as the DDI, the Corporate Leadership Council, Deloitte and the Center for Creative Leadership.[208] Figure 8.4 specifically demonstrates the thinking of the Center for Creative Leadership.

I. Strategy Alignment and Communication

1. Business Strategy Alignment
The leadership development strategy is developed and revised based on business strategy.
Maturity Level 1 2 3

2. Integrated Leadership Strategy
The leadership development strategy aligns with all other drivers of leadership effectiveness (e.g., recruitment, compensation, succession management).
Maturity Level 1 2 3

3. Values Alignment
The leadership development strategy aligns with the organization's values, and rewards and recognizes leaders for demonstrating them.
Maturity Level 1 2 3

4. Executive Engagement
Senior line executives are involved in the creation and execution of the leadership development strategy.
Maturity Level 1 2 3

II. Leadership Needs Assessment

5. Future-Focused Needs Assessment
The organization identifies leadership capabilities required for current and future organizational success.
Maturity Level 1 2 3

6. Leadership Capability Audits
The organization continuously assesses current and future leaders on business-critical competencies and knowledge.
Maturity Level 1 2 3

7. High-Potential Talent Identification
The organization identifies individuals with the ability, aspiration, and engagement to succeed at more senior levels.
Maturity Level 1 2 3

8. Retention Risk Tracking
The organization identifies (and mitigates against) leaders at risk of unwanted attrition.
Maturity Level 1 2 3

9. Leadership Segmentation
The organization prioritizes key leadership segments and critical capability gaps.
Maturity Level 1 2 3

10. Individualized Development Planning
Leaders have high-quality individual development plans that align to organizational and individual development needs.
Maturity Level 1 2 3

III. Development Planning and Delivery

11. Experiential Learning
The organization facilitates and encourages experiential learning (e.g., stretch roles) as one of the primary tools to develop leadership capabilities.
Maturity Level 1 2 3

12. Social Learning
The organization encourages and facilitates formal and informal social learning (e.g., relationships) as part of the leadership development strategy.
Maturity Level 1 2 3

13. Leadership Mobility
The organization facilitates and supports cross-organizational leadership mobility.
Maturity Level 1 2 3

14. Leader-Led Development
Senior leaders are held accountable for developing rising leaders.
Maturity Level 1 2 3

15. Knowledge Transfer
The organization ensures that key knowledge is transferred effectively from leaders leaving the organization.
Maturity Level 1 2 3

16. Leadership Transitions
The organization supports leaders during upward transitions into more senior roles.
Maturity Level 1 2 3

17. Targeted Formal Programs
Where appropriate, the organization offers high-quality formal leadership development programs that enable leaders to apply what they learn and use the right mix of delivery methods (e.g., classroom, eLearning).
Maturity Level 1 2 3

IV. Evaluation and Accountability

18. Strategy Assessment
The organization identifies and tracks metrics that capture the execution and impact of its leadership development strategy.
Maturity Level 1 2 3

19. Program Evaluation
The organization rigorously measures the effectiveness and impact of individual leadership programs.
Maturity Level 1 2 3

20. Strategy Governance
There is clear accountability for ownership and execution of the leadership development strategy.
Maturity Level 1 2 3

Leadership Development Strategy Outcomes

Leadership Effectiveness: Our leadership team has the capabilities required to manage the business effectively.

Succession Pipeline: Our organization has a strong bench of candidates for key leadership positions.

Leadership Confidence: Our employees believe in our leaders, and believe that they demonstrate our core values.

Leadership Brand: We are recognized internally and externally as a top organization for developing leaders.

Individualized Development Planning

Which level best describes your organization's maturity at Individualized Development Planning?

☐ Level 1: Individual development plans for leaders are used inconsistently throughout the organization.

☐ Level 2: Most leaders have development plans, but they vary in quality and are inconsistently applied. Leaders receive somewhat useful support from their managers.

☐ Level 3: Nearly all leaders have high-quality development plans that are aligned with organizational and individual needs. Leaders actively apply their development plans with useful support from their managers.

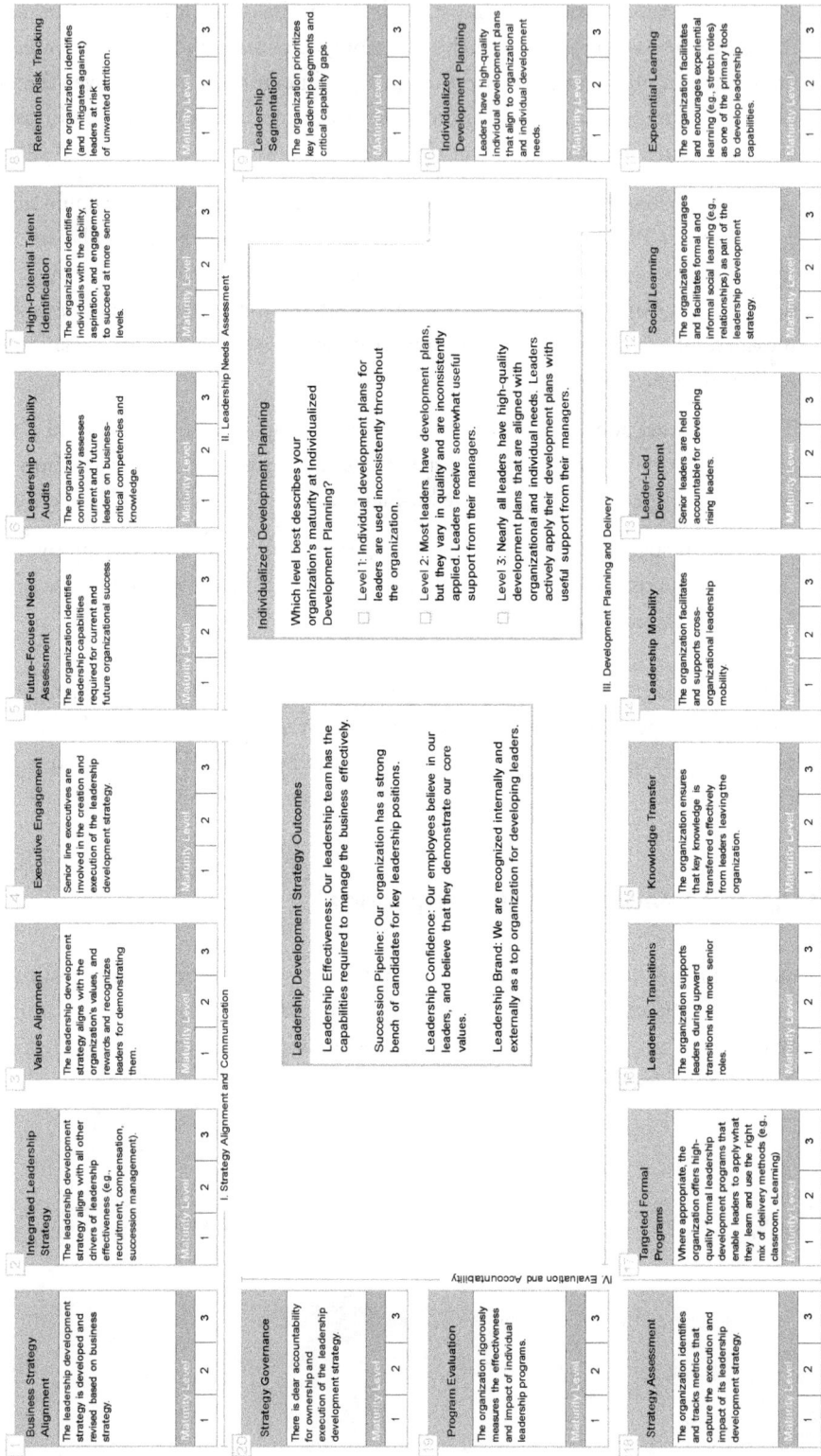

Figure 8.4 Integrated Leadership Strategy model: Center for Creative Leadership

The common themes running through all the approaches identified in our literature review are:

1. Leadership impact begins with a leadership strategy clearly linked to the overall business strategy.

2. An outcome of the leadership strategy is a clearly defined set of behavioural expectations of leadership (sometimes also called a leadership brand or a leadership culture).

3. Current and potential leaders are assessed against the leadership strategy and then developed.

4. This should serve to create a leadership landscape (capacity, style, demographics etc).

5. This should serve to create measureable value linked to the business strategy.

This logical flow is presented in figure 8.5.

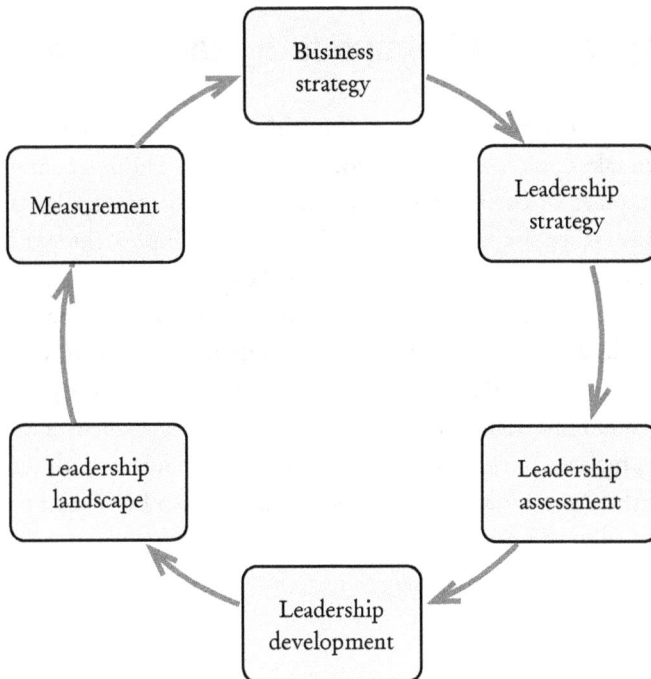

Figure 8.5 Integrated Leadership Strategy model

Summary

From our perspective, the application of a benefits-realisation approach is different from a typical ROI approach from both a philosophical and practical perspective. From our own and client experiences, building such an approach takes time, as you require:

- conversations to create alignment on philosophy

- adjustment of practices to drive integration

- consistency of all people- and talent-management practices

It requires the learning and development department to take a perspective on

- context – business brand, strategy, external strategic drivers

- purpose – specific advantages to be achieved through building talent excellence

- process – specific formal and informal processes of talent identification and development

- content – ensuring that all content plugged into processes is fit for purpose

And lastly it provides a powerful way to communicate the benefits of talent excellence to a range of stakeholders.

Measuring leadership impact: a practical approach

Having now walked a journey with you to explain our own mental models and thinking, the next section takes you through a practical application. This is a combination of our work over a number of client systems looking at how to measure leadership impact. Our approach is rather simple and adopts the logic that inputs entered into a process or practice will lead to specific outputs, and that these will result in specific value-added outcomes. In line with this logic we accept that **investment** (inputs) in leadership excellence must lead to demonstrable business **benefits** (results). In order for this to happen, we have to ensure that the right capacity is developed (**outputs/deliverables** achieved). To build the right capacity, our leadership assessment and development processes and **practices** must be relevant to the strategic intent with leadership. This in turn means that our **thinking** about leadership needs to be aligned to our strategic intent. Conceptually, this can be illustrated as in figure 8.6:

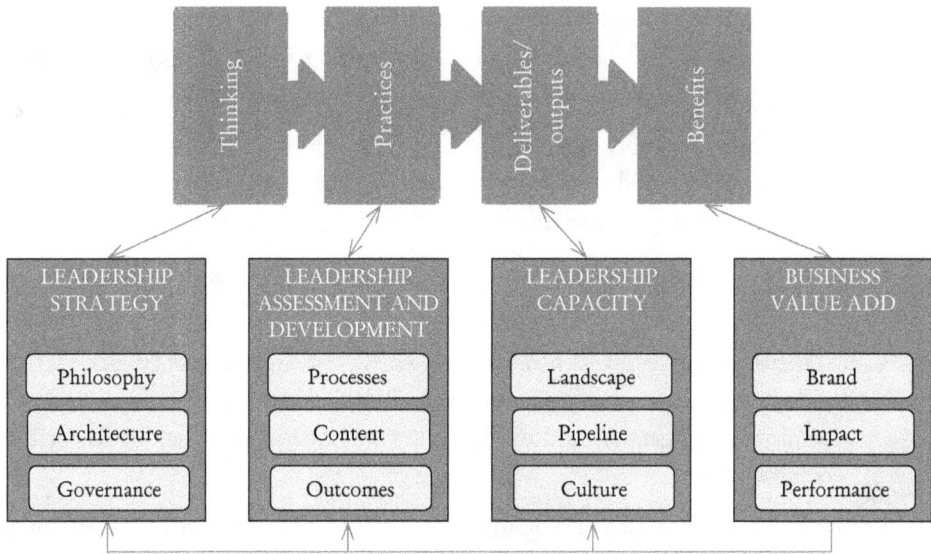

Figure 8.6 Leadership impact conceptual model

The features of the model are:

1. Leadership strategy should be defined within the context of the overall business strategy, which should as a matter of course include an assessment and articulation of the leadership drivers inherent in or assumed by such a business strategy. A leadership strategy in turn should be explicit about aspects such as:

    a. how we think about leadership, meaning the desired leadership philosophy (or brand), including the desired leadership behaviours at different levels of leadership

    b. architecture, meaning how we segment leadership levels, how we allocate resources to the leadership strategy and how we structure both interventions and delivery channels

    c. governance, such as budget allocated to leadership development practices, leadership selection rules, leadership accountabilities etcetera

2. Leadership assessment and development practices should be based on the desired leadership brand, and should consider specifically:

    a. the assessment and development processes

    b. definition of the appropriate assessment and development content (interventions and technologies)

    c. clearly defined outcomes of assessment and development. From a development perspective, this is clearly where the traditional thinking about evaluation of learning such as through the Kirkpatrick and Philips models comes into its own.

3. Leadership capacity, which is the level at which one finally sees the impact (or benefits realisation) of the execution of the leadership strategy. It typically includes aspects such as:

    a. leadership landscape, meaning the degree to which a leadership community has been established that is able to create collective alignment and focus, and whether or not the leadership community is regarded as trustworthy

    b. pipeline, meaning succession for key roles and/or people, nurturing of high-potential individuals, leader mobility and risk cover

    c. leadership culture, which may be equated to the experience of internal stakeholders of the desired leadership brand. It therefore extends beyond employee engagement and by definition includes aspects such as leadership community.

4. For each of these domains of measurement, specific measures and/or metrics may exist at the strategic, tactical, operational and quality levels. These "levels" of measurement can loosely be seen as being related to the principles of levels of work or the matrix of working relationships, as defined by Elliot Jaques[209] and others.

5. For each of the measures and/or metrics, one would also need to establish their specific relevance to and definition of each of the different leadership segments (executive, management, supervisory) as the assumption cannot be made *ab initio* that they are identical.

Measures and metrics: the search for the Holy Grail

In our experience, defining measures and metrics is like the search for the Holy Grail. Embarking on this process, though vital, is not easy, and companies often do one of two things: 1) they measure easy-to-track metrics with no real meaning or 2) at the opposite extreme, they search for the "perfect answer" and consequently make little progress.

In the rest of the section we suggest a thinking framework to get you started. This can be used to stimulate your own thinking on measuring leadership impact.

Leadership strategy

Philosophy
- The philosophy measure may include elements of:
  - o the degree to which there is clarity on the leadership brand/value framework that indicates the required leadership behaviours (leadership competency model) that should be lived internally and externally
  - o the degree to which the leadership strategy aligns the shared attitudes, values, beliefs and practices (at all levels in the organisation), to drive the leadership brand and behaviours

Architecture
- The architecture measure may include elements of:
  - o integration of the strategy and the architecture
  - o link between the leadership framework and development practices implemented
  - o degree to which the required leadership behaviours are aligned to the leadership brand/values identified

Governance
- The governance measure may include elements of:
  - o internal rules that govern leadership acquisition, development and promotion
  - o the extent to which leadership is held accountable for critical leadership actions
  - o budget availability for leadership practices

Leadership assessment and development practices

Process
- The process measure may include elements of:
  - o leadership assessment and development process efficiency
  - o flexibility of the process

Content
- The content measure may include elements of:
  - o relevance of development programmes
  - o level appropriateness of learning solutions

Outcome
- The outcome measure may include elements of:
  - o participant reaction and degree of participation
  - o perception of the value-add of the practices
  - o changes in behaviour and improvement in performance

Leadership capacity

Landscape
• The landscape measure may include elements of:
    o   the degree of collaboration across the various levels
 	
Pipeline
• The pipeline measure may include elements of:
    o   ability to "cover" critical leadership positions from within
 	
Culture
• The culture measure may include elements of:
    o   observable and consistent leadership behaviour that is aligned to the values
    o   employee engagement

Business benefit

Strategic
• The strategic measure may include elements of:
    o   stakeholder perceptions of leadership excellence
 	
Tactical
• The tactical measure may include elements of:
    o   leadership responsiveness to changing business context
Operational
• The operational measure may include elements of:
    o   people and nonpeople cost efficiencies
 	
Execution
• The execution measure may include elements of:
    o   quality of outputs and compliance/adherence to standards

In chapter 7 we spoke about both the formal and informal aspects of building leadership capacity. In our experience organisations are quite adept at defining measures and metrics for formal leadership solutions, but often don't know where to start in defining some measures of informal practices. We thought it prudent to stimulate some thinking here as well, as leadership development cannot take place from a formal perspective only.

Learning framework for business benefits realisation

As discussed in the previous chapter, new strategies to improve organisational leadership development capacity increasingly favour approaches emphasising experiential, informal and self-directed learning. This does bring to mind the question of how we measure the leadership development aspect of the bigger leadership scorecard. The first temptation here is to focus on the development of the leader and not of the collective leadership community.

When attempting to measure informal learning we suggest following our recipe mentioned in chapter 7:

Table: 8.1:

Purpose	Why do we want to measure informal learning? What will we do with the information?
Process	What process will we follow? Where will we engage our employees? How does technology (eg learning portal, wiki) impact our process?
Content	What specific measures and metrics can we consider? How will we obtain the data? What questions do we need to ask?

You may find the following framework useful when considering the measurement of leadership development only.

Table: 8.2:

Component	Formal learning measures	Informal learning measures
Learning process	• extent of other leaders' involvement in the process • horizontal and vertical integration of the process	• extent of other leaders' involvement in the process • extent to which participants feel their participation has been worthwhile • horizontal and vertical integration of the process
Learning content	• appropriateness in terms of alignment to competencies, leadership brand and work complexity	• extent to which people contribute to content creation • appropriateness in terms of alignment to competencies, leadership brand and work complexity

Component	Formal learning measures	Informal learning measures
Learning support tools	• satisfaction/usefulness of learning support tools	• the types of activity they engage in • satisfaction with the technology
Facilitators/ Coaches	• facilitator effectiveness	• coach effectiveness
Impact	• improvements to competencies and skill sets • leadership behaviour change • recommendation for others to attend	• improvements to competencies and skill sets • leadership behaviour change • recommendation for others to attend

Summary

Put simply, the literature reviewed seems to suggest that the purpose of measuring leadership impact broadly has two points of departure. On the one hand is the approach that attempts to determine to what degree leadership development processes and programmes have some demonstrable "value". The typical and well-known approaches of Kirkpatrick and Philips are examples of this approach, both of whom at some point in their models move to the second approach, which is to shift the focus away from development per se and towards the actual business benefits realised.

Whilst there may be some broad consensus on how the "value" of leadership development may be calculated, there is significantly less clarity and consensus on how the business benefit of leadership itself may be determined. The reason for this lack of clarity is that the answer depends on what question we are asking, and of whom.

In the next and final chapter we share with you a number of case studies in various organisations. We have been fortunate to collaborate with some very extraordinary individuals in building their own leadership communities.

Chapter 9

From dream to action

Anton Verwey and Letitia van der Merwe

❄

"Time ripens all things; no man is born wise." – **M de Cervantes**

"Experience is what you get when you didn't get what you wanted. And experience is often the most valuable thing you have to offer."
– **Randy Pausch,** *The Last Lecture*

In this book we explored ways and means to build a corporate leadership community. In essence, we are suggesting that:

- The competitive landscape for business has changed dramatically, and will continue to do so.

- This requires us to adopt different strategies with different behaviours.

- This in turn requires a different view of leaders as individuals, when stepping into their roles and when being part of the broader leadership community.

- All of the above means we have to rethink our leadership capacity-building processes and practices.

The absolute bottom line is that the very traditional approaches to leadership talent identification and development processes will not build the leadership capacity we need to be successful in the future. Clearly, this also places particular demands on the leadership development functions in organisations. Hopefully, this book also provides some new perspectives for these professionals.

In this final chapter we share with you some case studies in terms of our practical experiences with clients. Our grateful thanks go to these clients for contributing so much to our understanding of how to create a leadership community. For us, there were two key lessons to be learnt:

- Find the leadership development processes in the system that already work, and build on them.

- There is no substitute for executive and senior leadership ownership.

Case 1: Changing the leadership mind-set

Our first example is of a client in the energy sector that specifically focused on building a leadership brand through leadership community. They shared with us the following.

Leadership philosophy

The client based their leadership philosophy on the following principles:

- To change a corporate culture rapidly, one needs to bring the preferred future culture into the present.

- Leadership is more a matter of courage and mind-set than of skills.

- Leadership is the responsibility of each and every individual in the team.

- Culture change requires leadership development as a sustained process approach, not just a series of quick interventions.

- For leadership, team and culture development to be successful one needs to bring everybody in the room into a learning space.

- A constructive culture requires values inclusion and co-creation of interdependent people with common goals.

Changing the leadership mind-set

To operationalise a changed (and changing) leadership mind-set, an awareness and integration of specific elements are necessary. Although it will never be linear but always systemic, it needs to start with strategy – deliberately addressing individual and collective mind-set change as a priority in the leadership strategy. Be upfront about the Inside-Out philosophy, meaning that all leadership development initiatives will focus on:

- me (leader) and what is driving my behaviour

- me stepping into the space of my team (me in my leadership role)

- me and other leaders and how I/we step into the collective organisational space (leadership culture)

It goes without saying that leadership strategy is aligned to organisational strategy and that the execution of leadership strategy will happen within a holistic, integrated logic. Table 9.1 contains some of the key aspects of such a leadership mind-set journey we have developed through practical application.

Table 9.1 The leadership mind-set journey

Key Aspects	Considerations
Leadership brand	Position the leadership brand as the invisible link between leader, team and organisational behaviour.
Be deliberate in the preparation of the leadership development team	What is our own mind-set and what behaviour is that driving? Have the required rigorous conversations and ensure that nothing is left to chance; reflect as much as required, before, during and after events.
Assessment of individual capability and competence	The use of scientific data to shape individual development plans and collective development initiatives remains important. Competence gaps serve as drivers for development solutions, while capability profiles support leadership talent management processes.
Architecting the development solutions	Adopt a clear and consistent Inside-Out philosophy, architecture and practice across different development solutions across the leadership pipeline. Start all development journeys with ME and what is driving my leadership behaviour (think differently so that I can do differently). Be clear on the experiential nature of the learning methodology – it is action, experiences and conversation that will break the "stuckness" of current mind-sets.
Choosing your learning development partners wisely	Do not compromise on the meeting of hearts and minds when selecting external partners. Find world-class specialists that deeply share the Inside-Out philosophy. Leave nothing to chance; collaborate extensively on the desired outcomes.

Key Aspects	Considerations
Development facilitation	The skill of the facilitator in identifying and addressing unconscious collusion/defensive behaviour and bringing the learning back to ME is of significant importance. Replication and continuously repeating the foundational supporting practices such as journalling, self-reflection and dialogue across the development pipeline are also of significant importance.
Architect and implement integrative development solutions with the objective of bringing the collective together and facilitating application of individual learning	A practical example is an intrateam solution that brings the leader and his or her team together, to work on real, day-to-day challenges and to merge parallel personal growth journeys. Similarly, architect interteam solutions are needed to facilitate conversations to remove barriers that affect interdependence across the value chain. Both solutions further reinforce the leadership brand as a conduit.
Continuous, deliberate and mindful learning	Position reflective practice as an enabler in the personal growth journey in building the "reflective mind-set" and in the collective team and culture space.

Case 2: Systemic leadership

In our second case we move to a company in the aviation industry, Global Load Control. The company's primary purpose is to provide remote weight- and balance-and-load-control services to the parent airline, as well as several other airline companies globally.

Building the leadership community

From its inception, the company has been challenged to position itself in such a way that it maintains its relevance as a unique subsystem operating within the broader systemic context of the parent organisation. While the company must always maintain a certain likeness to its parent company, it must also continually cultivate its own unique culture and identity, which set it apart as an independent entity and prevent redundancy.

From a leadership philosophy perspective, this thinking around culture has been manifested in certain deliberate decisions being taken that are aimed at maintaining a careful balance between "similarity" and "uniqueness" over time and in the midst of continual environmental changes. Many of these decisions have involved the creation of an integrated leadership community that is able to operate effectively and flexibly as a network among networks, and advocate certain core company values across geographically and culturally diverse contexts.

As such, the leadership community is tasked with ensuring that the company continues to offer a long-term value proposition to its parent company. With a growing trend of outsourcing remote services to Asia, the company stands firm in its belief that its people are what set it apart. As such, they are not only capable of offering their services at rates competitive with those in Europe, but are able to do so without compromising quality because of the high calibre of people they employ.

From a leadership perspective, the company's leadership team actively strives to create the future collectively and to contribute positively to the success of the societies of which they are a part. They view a leader as someone who is able to grow the capacity and ability of their people beyond that which they previously thought possible; therefore they strive to empower each individual to reach his or her full potential. This means that individuals are consciously seen as the most valuable assets of the company and that employees are chosen not only on the basis of pure talent, but also on potential, even if that potential has not yet revealed itself.

What is clear in this company is that building a leadership community is a very deliberate and mindful application. In their sense, community is a cultural organism that is more than those individual human beings of whom it is made up. Culture consists of all those things, including the actions and beliefs which human beings learn, which make them human. Culture includes learned behaviour, and is stored and transmitted by symbols.

Deliberate actions to build a systemic leadership community

Although the company holds their employees to extremely high standards, as a company they are also willing to go the extra mile in developing and empowering their team. The leadership team has therefore implemented several enablers that contribute to embedding a leadership community and ideal culture. Some of these core enablers are discussed in the following section.

Recruitment and selection for potential

In today's globalised, competitive environment, companies often refer to "the war for talent". In comparing the acquisition of talent to a war, the conscious or unconscious assumption is that talent is a scarce resource that is difficult to source, secure and retain. The aim is therefore to develop recruitment and selection procedures that attract a scarce commodity that would otherwise be absorbed by competitors. In quite the opposite way, the organisation advocates a view that talent is an abundant resource just waiting to be discovered in the labour market. When hiring employees, leadership therefore aims to attract not only talent that has already been developed, but also potential talent that requires investment and refinement. In adopting this approach, the company believes that it opens itself up to an entire untapped market that other companies are failing to consider and facilitates a process whereby individuals are able to reach a level of personal and professional success which they previously never believed possible. In the process, the company also creates a workforce that is engaged and committed to contributing their best to the business.

Training and development opportunities at all levels

Consistent with their philosophy of recruiting and selecting for potential, the organisation believe that all employees across all levels of the business should have access to opportunities that allow for further development. They have therefore developed an extensive professional training and development programme, which allows employees across the business access to a variety of courses and programmes that cater for a variety of interests and learning styles. Even in instances where individuals wish to pursue a certification or degree in a field that is not directly related to the business, the company will support this endeavour as long as the individual will be able to apply the acquired knowledge within the company or inject new ways of thinking into the culture. They realise that individuals have their own personal goals and visions, and they want to make it possible for individuals to live out their ambitions within the company environment.

Absolute individual accountability

The organisation's senior leadership believes that individuals generally want to contribute to the overall success of the business and aim to make a lasting difference through the work that they do on a daily basis. As such, in the company are entrusted with a great deal of responsibility and are well versed in the unique contribution that they make to the company as a whole. Individuals are also expected to raise concerns or recommend improvements at all levels of the business.

By enabling individuals to take full accountability for their work outputs, the company has created a system whereby open communication occurs at a fast pace. Knowledge sharing is a key value and employees are expected to learn from one another and contribute to the growth and sustainability of the business in a proactive way. They believe that their flat organisational structure has made them dynamic and flexible in responding to the changing needs of the environment, and has allowed them to adapt in ways that other companies are unable to.

Creating space for individuals to excel professionally and personally

While it expects continuous high performance from its employees, the company also realises the importance of life outside work and has therefore implemented policies that promote work–life balance. In allowing employees space for their personal lives, leadership found that individuals are mentally present in their work rather than simply being a "bum on a seat".

From the above it can be seen that in order to realise the strategic intent and business strategy, the company believes that leadership which creates an enabling culture will get people to perform optimally.

Embedding the leadership culture

The company's approach and culture seem to be well embedded in senior and middle management. The challenge remains not only to entrench the thinking, but also to live the desired culture, throughout the organisation. According to the current general manager, their culture is multi-layered. There are pockets of extremely hierarchical elements, but predominantly this culture is about collaboration and collective leadership. The second challenge is that this systemic approach to leadership and culture is still very much driven by senior management. Even though it is understood and supported by middle management, the question remains as to how well this spirit will survive in the absence of senior management.

Case 3: Building a leadership community

Our next case is an organisation within the retail industry where the teams evolved over a number of years. This again illustrates that building a leadership community takes time. Fairly dramatic competitive positioning and organisation architecture changes led to a renewed resolve at executive level to rethink the entire leadership development strategy. In very broad terms, the HR community introduced a deliberate process to address the following aspects:

- defining a leadership stance – the leadership development strategy

- defining the leadership identification and development processes

- defining and developing the leadership development content[210]

In the rest of this section, each of these aspects is explored in more detail from a very practical perspective. This section concludes with a brief explanation of how implementation was driven.

Defining the leadership brand

In early 2008 we were formally requested to participate in the redesign of the leadership development programmes. In fact this involved much more than a simple "upgrade" of leadership development programmes, and such a process needed to be tightly embedded into a broader organisation culture transformation process. Specifically, by thinking through levels of work and the nature of organisation's culture, it was understood that the new breed of leadership would need to embrace a very different level of complexity and lead in very different ways to the traditional approach in retail.

It was also understood at an executive level that the organisation needed to engage itself in a series of conversations about its leadership stance, rather than merely simplistically reviewing leadership development content. Leadership development became one of the five key strategic initiatives owned by HR.

In our approach to this strategic initiative, a number of key principles were established:

- For every aspect worked on we would be specific about purpose, process and content.

- We would be as inclusive and collaborative as possible in everything we did, as the process of redeveloping leadership development could then itself model the culture transformation.

- We would be deliberate in communicating[211] as much as we could about the purpose, process and content.[212]

As a point of departure, the core team agreed the following:

Purpose	The purpose of redefining the entire leadership development philosophy was to create the leadership capacity (the right numbers of leaders with the required capability and competencies) to support the achievement of the business strategy.
Process	To achieve this purpose, the process of leadership development should embrace an integrated approach to 1) the definition of leadership for the group, 2) assessment of capability and competence and 3) targeted development of leadership at all levels.
Content	To ensure that the process drives the achievement of our purpose, the content of leadership development should go beyond formal workshops and include aspects such as informal learning, coaching and mentoring, creating a common leadership language, links to other strategic initiatives, and so forth.

Conceptual design

As a first step, the core team decided to put together a detailed leadership development strategy document. The purpose of this document was to create a formal record of the thinking of the organisation so that specific interventions could be properly contextualised at a later stage. In terms of the content of the document, we set up a proposed structure and populated the various sections with existing content where we could. In terms of process, we decided to let the organisation supply the remaining content for each section of the document.

As a second step, the approach, including a high-level draft version of the leadership framework, was discussed with the executive team. One of the most significant conclusions from this conversation was that a key issue was raising the level of complexity of all divisions to one of strategic development. Some of the issues explored in this conversation also centred on the degree to which divisions had (or should have) unique leadership cultures, the stages at which leadership development becomes a corporate rather than divisional function, and the fact that assessment of competence should be done in a manner that allows individuals to take ownership of their development while maintaining their personal dignity. Some specific suggestions were also made about the leadership framework itself.

Armed with the leader development strategy document, the core team could now turn its attention to developing the content of the strategy.[113] Broadly, this fell into three specific domains, namely:

- articulating leadership competencies at different levels of complexity
- translating the behaviours defined for the competencies into curriculum specifications
- setting up the various leadership assessment processes

The manner in which these activities were sequenced in the project is outlined in figure 9.1.

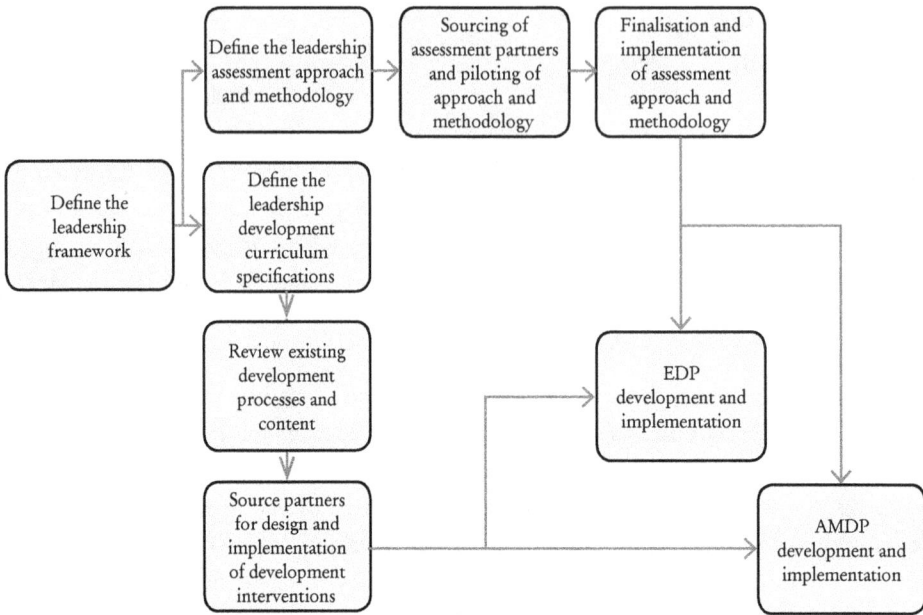

Figure 9.1 Project activities

The leadership framework

As a first step, the draft leadership competence framework (see figure 9.2) was enhanced by an external project team to:

- Define for each competency in the framework the required behaviour at different levels of complexity.

- Define the degrees of proficiency for each competency within each level of complexity.

- Highlight so-called "red flag" behaviours for each competency.

Business results

Business direction setting	Driving execution	Engaging people
• Thinking strategically • Business acumen • Market orientation • Influencing others • Integrity and values • External networking	• Acting strategically • Information processing • Judgement and decision making • Resource management • Customer orientation • Risk management • Programme and project management	• Communication • Knowledge and innovation management • Internal networking • Talent management • High performance teaming • Engaging diversity • Leading change

Experience (Record performance)	Know-how (Specialist knowledge/skills)

Personal characteristics

• Taking action • Courage and confidence/conviction/candour • Self-insight • Wisdom	• Emotional maturity • Personal resilience • Drive and energy

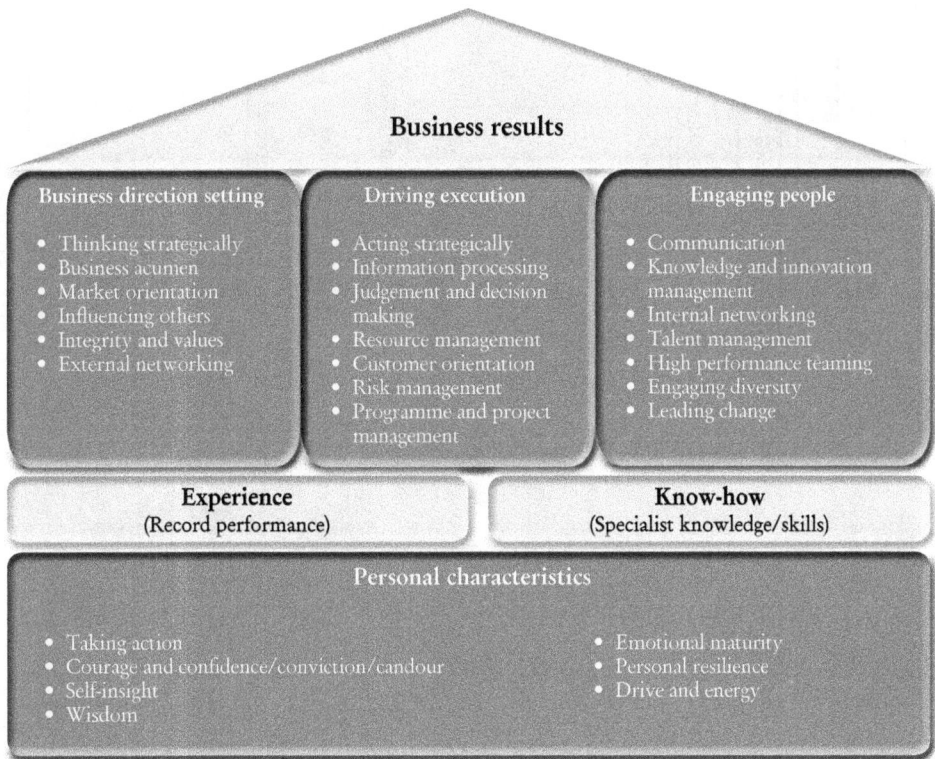

Figure 9.2 Leadership framework

The result of this process led to a draft document of behavioural descriptors for each competency across different levels of complexity. Figure 9.3 illustrates what the end result of this process looked like.

Figure 9.3 Example of behavioural descriptors

Labels (pointing to parts of the table):
- Competency
- Definition
- Purpose
- Degree of proficiency
- Type of complexity
- Behavioural descriptor
  - Know
  - Manage
  - Do
  - Contribute
- Red flag behaviour

Business acumen

Definition: Knows how JD Group businesses work. Knowledgeable in current and possible future policies, practices, trends, and information affecting his/her business. Is aware of how strategies and tactics work in the marketplace.

Purpose: Leadership effectiveness is often judged by an individual's displayed business competence. A leader seeking credibility and trust will invest in the development and of commercial and financial acumen.

	Know	Manage	Degree of proficiency	Contribute
Strategic development	Cannot needs develop the business model and principles and position JD Group strategically within the market.	Needs guidance in developing the business model and principles and position JD Group strategically within the market.	Develops the business model and principles and position JD Group strategically within the market.	Positions the business in such a way that the organisation is an industry leader in terms of generally accepted business indicators.
	Focuses on limited business drivers neglecting the impact on the overall business.	Understands the relevance of all business drivers but needs guidance to integrate these.	Takes all business drivers and the strategy into account in terms of the budgeting process and can draw up a budget for at least 5 financial years.	Translates strategy into current and future expenditure needs and monitoring costs and risk in line with corporate governance principles.
Good practice	Focuses only on one or two factors within business processes.	Understands the relationship between all the major factors of the business processes but is able to action only some of these.	Identifies and monitors internal effectiveness and efficiency dynamics which influences achievement of business goals and formulates appropriate tactics.	Generates and implements innovative processes to reduce costs and/or optimise profitability.
	Is not aware of the procedures and principles available to guide the budgeting process.	Struggles to manage budget within the parameters set before hand and needs extra funds at times.	Budgets optimally by weighing up costs, risks and potential returns on expenditure within all company parameters.	During current and future budgetary cycles he/she continuously looks for ways to leverage off additional cost savings and/or improved returns.
Service	Ignorant of business principles.	Needs guidance in applying basic business principles.	Understands basic business principles and how to they relate to and inform good customer service.	Identifies and monitors internal effectiveness and efficiency dynamics which influences achievement of business goals.
	Does not see the need to conduct cost/benefit analysis.	Needs guidance in conducting cost/benefit analysis.	Conduct cost/benefit analysis to guide operational decision-making for quality service delivery.	Budgets optimally by weighing up costs, risks and potential returns on expenditure within all company parameters.
Red flag behaviour	Fails to see commercial implications of actions. Relies on gut instinct to the exclusion of logic and hard data. Fails to identify business opportunities. Maintains the business status quo.			

Defining the leadership identification and development processes

As can be seen from figure 9.1, the definitions of the leadership assessment and development interventions and processes were run in parallel.

Leadership assessment

An expert panel in the assessment field was put together and given an extensive briefing on the leadership development strategy and the leadership framework. The key issues were to help this expert group understand at a very deep level not only the "technical" matching of assessment approaches and methodologies to the leadership framework, but also the fundamental people and leadership philosophy underpinning the entire leadership development strategy.

As an outcome of this phase, a set of recommendations for assessment approaches and methodologies was formulated, as well as a set of governance guidelines which also became part of the leadership development strategy document. In effect, the recommendations included:

- assessment of capabilities such as cognitive abilities and leadership personality profiles
- assessment of leadership behaviour through a company-specific development centre
- 360° assessments based on the leadership framework

Perhaps more importantly, a key principle adopted was that all forms of assessment had to be integrated into one feedback process, so that individuals participating in such processes could take personal ownership of the information and be empowered to make better decisions for themselves about their development and their careers. At a practical level, this also meant that we had to work with the selected assessment providers to ensure that their very different processes could be seamlessly integrated.

One of the most significant aspects of the final leadership assessment process was a decision taken that the entire executive team would also participate in the process. It was agreed that although the process may not necessarily provide significant personal value to this group from a developmental perspective, the intention was for this group to be seen to be modelling the way.

Leadership development

In parallel to the definition of the assessment processes outlined above, the design and development of the leadership development content took place (see figure 9.1). A significant decision formalised at this stage was to review the leadership development process in its entirety so that continuity could be achieved across levels of leadership, in line with both levels of work and the leadership pipeline. Practically, this meant 1) that the existing programmes would in all likelihood not continue and 2) a lower-level leadership development programme would also have to be developed, as it had not existed fully up to this point.

As a first step, the leadership behaviours as defined in the leadership framework were translated into curriculum specifications by a leadership development subject-matter expert group. The specifications were then workshopped with the project team, and then submitted to the steering committee for ratification. Secondly, all existing leadership development material was sourced from the company and compared to the curriculum specifications to determine what material needed to be scrapped, changed or developed from scratch. Thirdly, some design principles for both content and process were agreed on. Amongst them were that there would be an executive-level programme (EDP – Executive Development Programme) and a middle management-level programme (AMDP – Advanced Management Development Programme); that the intervention flow would adopt an "inside-out" approach; and that both programmes should be certified by a tertiary-level institution (see figure 9.4).

Defining and developing the leadership development content

Although this was touched on in the preceding section, it might still be valuable to explore in more detail the actual leadership development content as it evolved during the design phase. Specifically, the manner in which the formal content described above fitted into a more encompassing leadership redefinition process illustrates how a much more systemic perspective to leadership development was taken (figure 9.4).

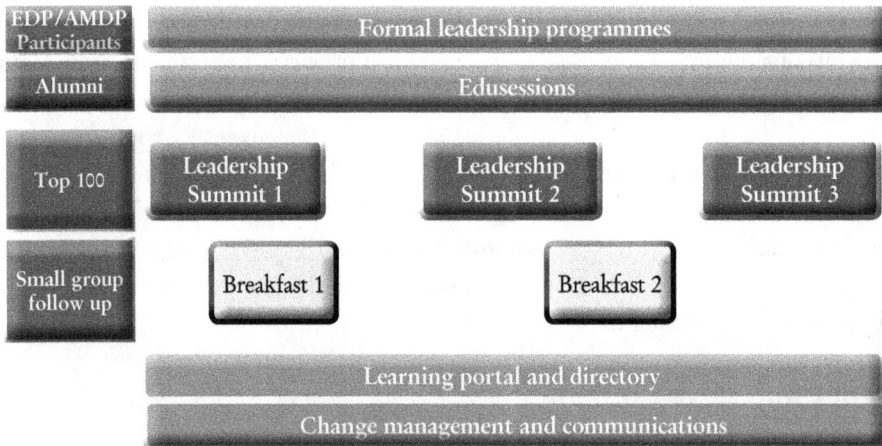

Figure 9.4 High-level leadership development process

As can be seen from figure 9.4, for both the EDP and the AMDP the formal content described earlier was only one part of a much larger leadership development process. As a planned and deliberate process, we decided that the entire leadership development process would consist of:

- personal learning through assessment

- personal, team and organisational learning through formal programmes (the EDP and AMDP)

- personal learning through access to a leadership learning directory[214]

- personal learning through access to an internal mentoring and external coaching

- organisational learning through leadership summits

- team learning through a variety of breakfast sessions

- specific and deliberate linking of leadership assessment and development to other talent management processes such as career and succession planning

- formalisation and extension of the leadership council to allow for group, division and chain perspectives on leadership capacity

In this entire process, we also consistently and frequently communicated the purpose, process and content of every single event, so that leadership became a topic with multiple conversations with various groups within the organisation.

Leadership summit

In keeping with the overall strategic intent of the leadership development strategy, we also constructed a deliberate process of having strategic leadership conversations. These conversations would be held as large group events with the top 100 leaders, with the express purpose of ensuring alignment around leadership across divisions, chains and service departments. By definition, these conversations would include all EDP participants, but exclude AMDP participants.

Based on our experience with other client systems, we decided up front that the leadership summits needed an overall theme, where each one of the summits could be an "episode" within a larger series or story. In addition, leadership summits should always demonstrate to participants the direct relationship between business strategy and leadership.

Breakfast conversations

Partly because we felt that we needed a process to extend awareness of the approach to leadership beyond the top 100, and also because we believed we needed a process to deliberately include the AMDP participants in additional processes, we structured a series of breakfast conversations. Given the design of the leadership summit outlined above, it became a fairly simple matter to design the breakfast conversation sessions. All that was really required was to condense each of the summit events into a two-hour event and provide the session coordinators with guidelines on what to do.

Clearly, the summit attendees would be the individuals taking the message of each summit back to their own divisions, chains or service departments by having similar breakfast sessions with their respective leadership teams. It was also decided to leave the specific format of these sessions to the judgement of the individual teams.

From dream to action – implementation

In an ideal world, all the design work described above would have been completed first, after which we would have implemented the solution in a stepwise manner. Reality is of course very different, and as noted more than once in this chapter, we had to overlap design and implementation throughout the process.[215] Having said this, I will do my best to tell the story of implementation in a sequential manner.

Launch

With the leadership framework completed, the assessment processes defined and the curriculum specifications finalised, we could now launch the entire leadership development process. A formal event was held to which the EDP and AMDP nominees and all senior leadership were invited. Great attention was given to creating an event that had the right level of gravitas. We explained the thinking behind the leadership development process to this audience. Emphasis was placed on how leadership excellence drives employee engagement, which in turn drives customer satisfaction and how this ultimately produces business results.

Summit One – levels and processes

We opted to have as the focus for the first leadership summit the element called Levels, Roles and Processes. The reason was simply that levels of work, although becoming well known at senior levels, still required conversations to ensure alignment. In addition, other HR strategic initiatives also required a higher level of understanding of the principles of levels of work amongst senior leadership. Quite fortuitously, this first summit took place within weeks of the implementation of the first phases of both the EDP and AMDP, and those participants had therefore already been exposed to the leadership landscape, the leadership framework and an orientation to levels of work theory.

As part of the process we used a video titled *Celebrate what's right with the world*, and then presented material on levels of work and leadership processes. This led to a very interactive session, with lots of questions being asked. Some specific questions on leadership capacity and roles were then explored.

We also asked the participants to complete a feedback form before departing, asking simple questions such as what they enjoyed most, what they learnt from each session and what they would change for following summits. More than 80 feedback forms were completed and returned, and the feedback was overwhelmingly positive. The journey of strategic leadership conversations had clearly begun!

EDP and AMDP

In September 2009 the formal leadership development programmes were initiated. The implementation was planned in a staggered manner, with the EDP preceding the AMDP by a week or two. As part of this process, we also had to decide up front on details such as branding of the programmes, templates for participant guides and facilitator slides, individual and group assignments, certification of the AMDP, and a host of other aspects.

Progressive conversations

A communication framework was developed with the purpose of supporting progressive leadership conversations. The framework became known as the integrated leadership excellence development process. Participants were informed that the business was undertaking this process to support the achievement of the stated strategic goals.

This inclusive process was cascaded through the business at many levels using:

- **Formal leadership programmes** – The EDP and AMDP are the new generation of formal programmes. They build on the proud history of leadership development, which has to date made a significant impact on the business through the contribution of all those who participated previously.

- **Edusessions** – In line with the commitment to keep developing leaders, and because of the belief that leadership development is an ongoing process, edusesssions are a key element of the process to ensure that all alumni keep up to date with the latest leadership development learnings.

- **Leadership summits** – Like the first summit, these sessions will allow the broader scope of leadership to meet at regular intervals to ensure that they keep driving leadership excellence in support of business strategy. The leadership summits are scheduled to take place every six months.

- **Breakfast sessions for leaders** – These more informal gatherings give leaders the opportunity to gather in smaller groups across chains and functions to celebrate successes and to allow them as leaders to take ownership of leadership conversations and development. These sessions will have a specific framework and will initially be guided by a facilitator. There will be two breakfast sessions a year, evenly spaced between the leadership summits.

- **Monthly sessions** – Regular monthly updates that take place in regular Exco or management meetings, where a regular agenda item will allow for robust two-way conversations about leadership within each area of expertise. Feedback from these sessions will be taken into consideration as we continue to design and develop integrated, tailor-made leadership development interventions.

- **Monthly session consolidation sessions** – These will take place the month before a breakfast session or a leadership summit. In these sessions leaders and their teams will have an opportunity to consolidate feedback they would like to take back to the bigger gatherings.

- The **learning portal and directory** and the **change management and communication** functions provide ongoing support to all the above-mentioned interventions.

Mentoring and coaching

As part of the process of enlarging the group of individuals who could effectively support the building of the leadership capacity, senior executives (many of whom had participated in the earlier RLDP programme) were asked to consider becoming mentors to the current EDP and AMDP participants. For this purpose, a mentoring skills programme was also introduced for mentors, and a detailed process designed and documented to ensure that such mentoring was appropriately governed and results-focused. For EDP participants, the option was also created to make use of external coaches if desired.

Website

Along with the processes already described, a leadership intranet website was created by the AMDP participants. On this site, the following documents were posted for use by EDP and AMDP participants, as well as the wider leadership community.

- the Leadership Development Strategy

- the Leadership Summit feedback report

- the Leadership Directory (which was updated every quarter with new material)

- course material from both the EDP and AMDP

Summary

As can be seen from this case, the implementation of the various initiatives in the leadership development space required significant attention to detail. We had to make sure that the sequencing and connections were clear, that time constraints were considered, business cycles kept in mind and so forth. The simple fact is that detailed project planning, dedicated project and communication support, and the ability of the entire team to react very quickly to every unforeseen challenge was instrumental in making this a truly exciting and remarkable journey.

Case 4: 70:20:10 Leadership development

Our final case is of a client in short-term insurance. The client wanted a true 70:20:10 learning model to implement their leadership brand promise. The 70:20:10 model for learning and development is based on research and observation carried out from the 1960s up to the present. Morgan McCall and his colleagues working at the Center for Creative Leadership (CCL) are usually credited with originating the 70:20:10 ratio. Various interpretations of the ratios exist, but in this case it was defined as:

- 70% of leadership development will happen on the job.

- 20% will happen through learning through others (social learning).

- 10% will happen through formal courses and reading.

Embracing and supporting the 70% and 20% was a new challenge for the client, and although the learning and development team were quite excited about the prospect of self-directed learning we knew that the challenges would surface at the implementation stage. Not all organisations are ready for a more self-directed approach to learning, so we chose an option we called "informal learning – but not unplanned and unstructured". In the next section we unpack some of steps we took as part of the process.

Starting with the end in mind

The purpose of the leadership development strategy was defined as follows:

- Ensure our leadership capacity-building strategy is aligned with the business strategy and our organisational values and adheres to the bigger MMI leadership framework.

- Establish and sustain an integrated leadership framework that displays our desired leadership brand.

- Ensure individual and collective leadership effectiveness in achieving our strategic objectives.

- Ensure consistent execution of the leadership framework.

The strategy contained the following elements, which were obtained through a variety of workshops and collaborations with employees:

- leadership philosophy and promise

- leadership development philosophy and key principles

- blended learning framework

- leadership development process with both vertical and horizontal alignment

- success/benefits criteria (linked to the talent criteria)

Figure 9.5 illustrates the integrated approach that was followed.

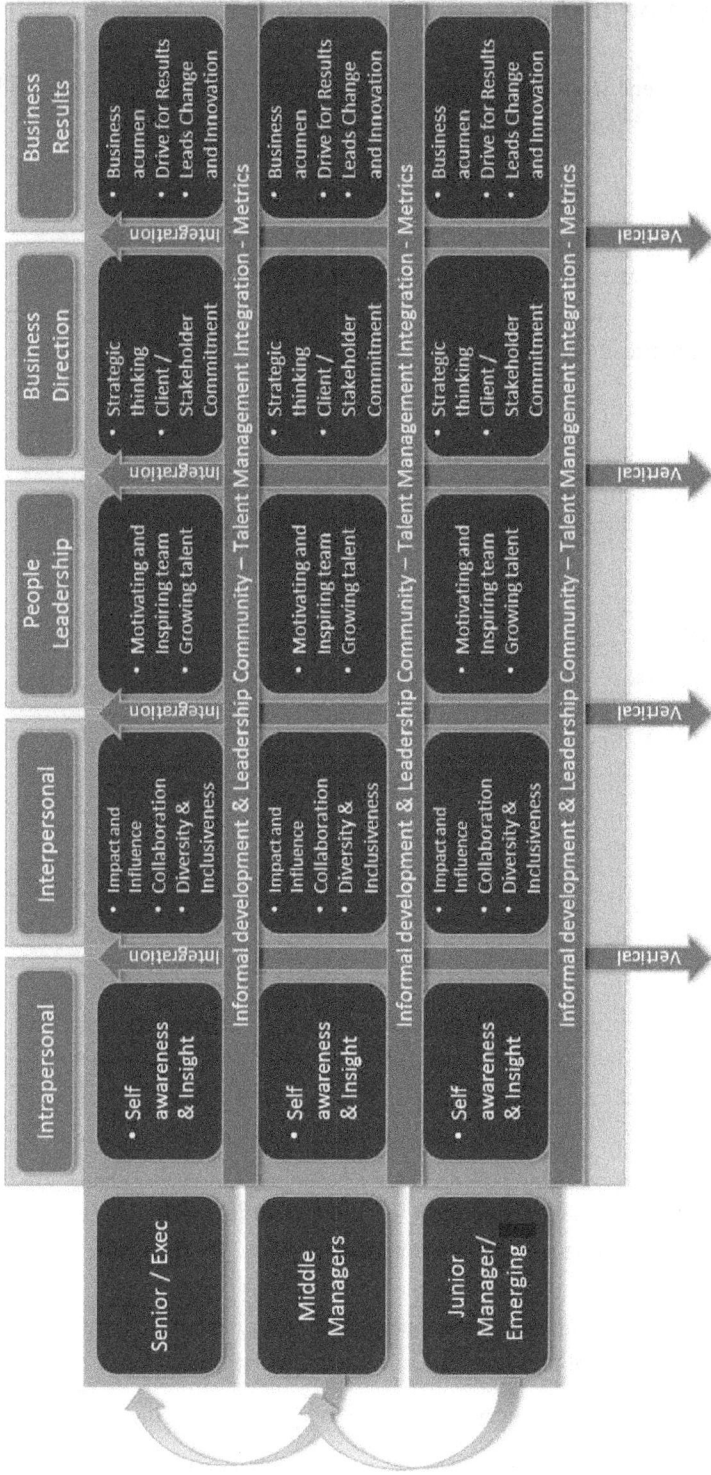

Figure 9.5 Integrated approach to leadership development

Building the learning process and curriculum

The leadership development strategy was then translated into a learning process and various curricula aimed at different leadership levels within the organisation.

Process

The learning process illustrated in figure 9.6 makes it clear that development had a dual purpose: 1) addressing the leadership brand promise and 2) individual development needs based on the competency framework.

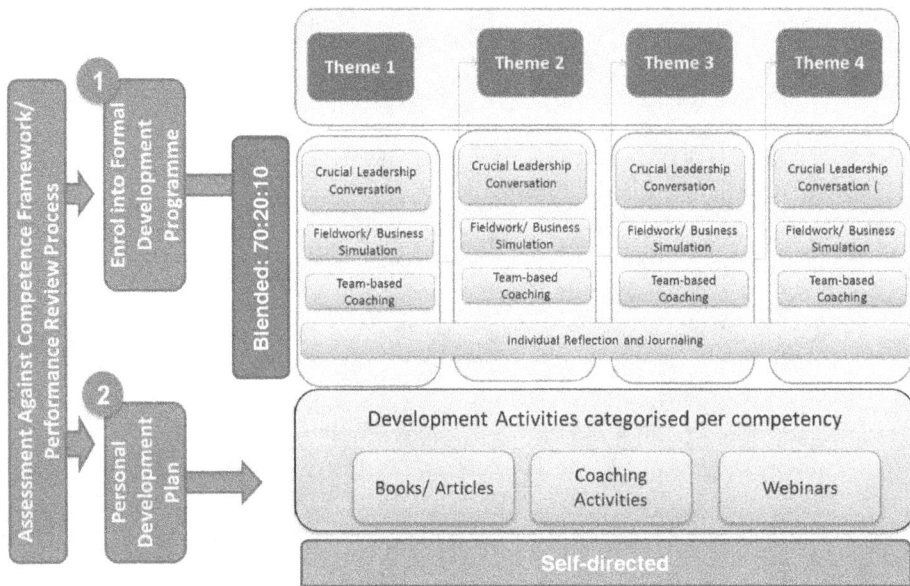

Figure 9.6 Learning process

Curriculum

The next step was the design of the curriculum for the different leadership groupings. It was fundamental that the learning solution incorporated the 70:20:10 principles:

- 70% from real life and on-the-job experiences, tasks and problem solving. This is the most important aspect of any learning and development plan.

- 20% from feedback and from observing and working with role models

- 10% from formal development

Below is an extract from the curriculum that was then translated into content and support tools.

Table 9.2: Theme 2: Intrapersonal

Learning Solution	Time Requirements	Tools / Templates
• Complete at least one on-the job activity with specific emphasis on communication and collaboration and discuss results with manager/ coach.	4 hours	• Learning directory
• Read two articles dealing with specifically diversity and communication and reflect lessons learnt in journal.	4 hours	• Resource directory and journal
• Attend a series of 4 x 1 hour sessions on how to have crucial conversations and deal effectively with conflict (attend the full workshop if not attended previously).	4 x 1 hours	• Source/ customise programme
• Develop a presentation and communication to peers aimed at how to create a motivating environment for your team. Share this with your manager/coach to get their feedback on the extent to which the communication will achieve its goal. (Utilise a team meeting).	4 hours	• Journal
Total classroom based: 4 hours Total self-study: Total interaction with peers/coach:		

Building content and the informal leadership development support tools

As previously stated, informal learning doesn't mean unstructured or unplanned. As part of the project various learning support tools were created to guide the leaders through the development journey, for example:

• coaching guidelines for managers who acted as coaches

• learning journey map

- learning directories inclusive of articles, on-the-job activities, learning communities clearly linked to the competencies and designed at the appropriate leadership pipeline level

An environment conducive to informal development

The organisation clearly understood that opportunities to engage in learning anytime or anywhere must address the issue of how to foster the desire for sustained and enduring learning. The learning and development team was very mindful that the design and implementation of this project needed to consider:

- providing opportunities to learn about something that is of interest and value

- providing learning events that are not prescriptive but fluid and flexible

- scaffolding difficult learning so that successes can be used to build further learning

- providing support, not answers

- taking a stance that the learning journey is the real outcome

- through senior leadership support, providing an environment that fosters collaboration and collegiality

- creating opportunities for self-reflection and self-appraisal

Over the years the organisation built a culture conducive to self-directed learning and development. They do not call it a leadership community, but the leadership culture is definitely characterised by what we have earlier called leadership brand enabling conditions.

- The organisation is clear on their leadership brand promise.

- Leadership is regarded as a responsibility and not as a right. Good leaders know that they have to earn the privilege of leading, and that that privilege needs to be earned on a perpetual basis.

- The leadership philosophy is not about power and greed, but about purpose – purpose in terms of people and profit (what they labelled "conscious capitalism").

- Leaders are required to achieve, without violating the values.

There are continuous formal and informal conversations about the leadership brand promise and the organisational values. There is a very clear partnership between the senior leadership team and the learning and development team. The CEO of the organisation plays a very clear and very collaborative role in terms of culture, leadership and values. By his own admission, one of his biggest challenges is not to intervene when he sees the values and leadership promise are not being lived. He encourages leaders at different levels of the organisation to rather have these conversations at an appropriate time.

Summary

Organisations have traditionally been and are still focused on developing individuals so that they can become better leaders; they put the emphasis on individual learning through the concepts of leader development and individual development plans. There seems to be a growing recognition that the emphasis should be on developing leadership as a collective. We envisage that the future will very likely be about developing leadership communities and networks of leaders; and therefore, when spotting and developing leadership talent, it clearly does not make sense to focus solely on the individual. The future challenge is to create a community of leaders able and willing to lead organisations through the turbulence of an increasingly complex world.

We find ourselves in uncharted waters, as very little formal writing about leadership community exists. We have described leadership community as the leaders at all levels of the organisation who consciously share a common purpose and who have a high degree of congruence, not only on the **how** of achieving the purpose, but also and more importantly the **why**. The existence of leadership community depends on the decisions taken at an organisational level as well as the choices and decisions of individuals. A very important requirement is now not only whether an individual leader has acquired all the competencies and skills required to fulfil the role of a leader, but whether the individual has the dexterity (agility) to deal with strategic, emotional and change-related aspects.

Leadership community building is indeed a process, and our work in various client systems has illustrated the need to take both a strategic long-term view on the process and a strong short-term implementation orientation.

References

American Express. 2011. *The Real ROI of Leadership Development: Comparing Classroom vs. Online vs. Blended Delivery*. Internal Publication.

April, K. A., MacDonald, R. & Vriesendorp, S. 2000. *Rethinking Leadership*. Cape Town: University of Cape Town Press.

Amagoh, F. 2009. Leadership development and leadership effectiveness. *Management Decision*, 47(6), 989-999.

Asree, S., Zain, M. & Razalli, M. R. 2010. Influence of leadership competency and organisational culture on responsiveness and performance of firms. *International Journal of Contemporary Hospitality Management*, 22(4), 500-516.

Avery, G. C. 2004. *Understanding Leadership: Paradigms and Cases*. London: Sage.

Avolio, B. J. & Kahai, S. S. 2003. Adding the "e" to leadership: How it may impact your leadership. *Organizational Dynamics*, 31, 325-338.

Avolio, B., Walumbwa, F. & Weber, T. J. (2009). Leadership: Current theories, research, and future directions. *Annual Review of Psychology*, 60, 421-449. Retrieved November 11, 2011, from http://digitalcommons.unl.edu/managementfacpub/37/.

Barrett, R. 1998. What is community? A sociological perspective. PhD. Retrieved January 25, 2014 from http://cec.vcn.bc.ca/cmp/whatcom.htm

Barrett, R. 2011. *Liberating the Corporate Soul: Building a Visionary Organisation*. Routledge: Butterworth-Heinnemann.

Bannister, A. 2008. Changing face of work. Retrieved June 25, 2009, from http://www.businesswings.co.uk /articles/The-changing-face-of-work.

Beck, D.E. & Cowan, C. 2005. Spiral Dynamics. Wiley-Blackwell; Reprint edition.

Ben-Hur, S & Kinley, K. 2012. Talent Intelligence: What you need to know to identify and measure talent. Jossey Bass.

Bhal, K. T., Bhaskar, A. U. & Ratnam, C. S. V. 2009. Employee reactions to M & A: Role of LMX and leader communication. Leadership & Organization Development Journal, 30(7), 604-624.

Bhaduri, A. 2011. *ROI of Leadership Development*. Accessed May 2012.

Bioss [Brunel Institute for Organisational and Social Studies]. 2009. *MCPA Training Manual*, Part 5 – Statistical Information, Amendment 14.

Bioss. 2010. *What Bioss Offers*: Tools. Retrieved October 7, 2012, from http://www.bioss.com/whatbiossoffers/tools/#cpa.

Bioss SA [Brunel Institute for Organisational and Social Studies Southern Africa]. 2005. *A summary of the statistical information on Career Path Appreciation (CPA) interview*. Johannesburg: Bioss Southern Africa.

Bishop, W. H. 2013. Defining the authenticity in authentic leadership. The Journal of Values-Based Leadership, 6, 1.

Block, L. 2003. The leadership-culture connection: An exploratory investigation. Leadership & Organization Development Journal, 24(6), 318-334.

Buch, K. & Rivers, D. 2001. TQM: The role of leadership and culture. Leadership & Organization Development Journal, 22(8), 365-371.

Bright, D. S., Alzola, M., Stansbury, J. & Stavros, J. M. (2011). Virtue ethics in positive organizational scholarship: An integrative perspective. Canadian Journal of Administrative Sciences, 28(3), 231-243.

Brooks, A. 1913. The Theory of Social Revolutions. http://www.gutenberg.org/files/10613/10613-h/10613-h.htm

Cameron, K. S. 2008a. Paradox in positive organizational change. *The Journal of Applied Behavioral Science*, 44(1), 7-24.

Cameron, K.S. 2008b. *Positive Leadership: Strategies for Extraordinary Performance*. San Francisco: Berrett-Koehler.

Cameron, K. 2010. Five keys to flourishing in trying times. *Leader to Leader*, Winter Issue, 45-52.

Cameron, K. S. & Caza, A. 2011. Contributions to the discipline of Positive Organizational Scholarship. *American Behavioral Scientist*, 47(6), 731-739.

Cameron, K. & Lavine, M. 2008. Making the impossible possible: Leading extraordinary performance: The Rocky Flats story. *Personnel Psychology*, 61, 208-212.

Cameron, K. S., Quinn, R. E. & DeGraff, J. 2006. *Competing Values Leadership: Creating Value in Organisations*. Northampton, MA: Edward Elgar Publishing.

Center for Creative Leadership. 2004. *Measuring the Impact of Leadership Development: How Can It Best Be Accomplished?*

Center for Creative Leadership. 2009a. *Evaluation Center*. EFMD Global Focus Volume 03 Issue 03.

Center for Creative Leadership. 2009b. Developing a leadership strategy a critical ingredient for organisational success. Global Organisational Leadership Development White Paper Series, May.

Charan, R., Drotter, S. & Noel, J. 2001. The Leadership Pipeline: How to Build the Leadership Powered Company. San Francisco: Jossey Bass.

Chemers, M. M. 200). Leadership, Change, and Organisational Effectiveness. Conference Proceedings of the Symposium on the Co-evolution of Technology-Business Innovations. San Jose, CA: IBM Almaden Research Center. Retrieved June 16, 2009, from http://www.almaden.ibm.com/coevolution/pdf/chemers_paper.pdf.

Cohen, E. & Sinha, A. 2008. Develop a winning Leadership Brand. Chief Learning Officer, 7(9), 66.

Cole, D, Boyatzis, R & McKee, A. 2004. *Primal leadership: the hidden driver of great performance*. Harvard Business School Press.

Collins, DB. 2001 *The effectiveness of managerial leadership development programs: a meta-analysis of studies from 1982-2001*. Louisiana State University.

Collins, J. 2001. *Good to Great*. London: Random House.

Conger, J. 1990. The dark side of leadership. *Organisational Dynamics*, Autumn 1990:44-55.

Corporate Leadership Council. 2010a. *Agilent's Leadership Effectiveness Analysis*.

Corporate Leadership Council. 2010b. *Anatomy of an Effective Leadership Development Strategy*.

Corporate Leadership Council. 2009. *Managing leadership performance risks*.

Corporate Leadership Council. 2010. *Improving Returns on Leadership Investments*

Corporate Leadership Council. 2014. http://www.ccl.org/leadership/pdf/research/LeadershipStrategy.pdf

Coverdale Global. 2011. *What is the ROI of leadership development?* Accessed May 2012.

Cubbon, A. 1969. Hawthorne talk in context. *Occupational Psychology*, 43, 111-128.

Dalrymple, J. 2000. From F. Winslow Taylor to W. Edwards Deming: Over a century of progress? Conference Proceedings of the 1st International Research Conference on Organisational Excellence in the Third Millennium. Fort Collins, CO: Colorado State University, Fort Collins Estes Park. Retrieved June 16, 2009, from http://mams.rmit.edu.au/35zkk9ztt0qn.pdf.

Day, DV. 2001. Leadership development: a review in context. *Leadership Quarterly*, 11(4):581-613.

De Jong, J. P. J. & Den Hartog, D. N. 2007. How leaders influence employees' innovative behaviour. European Journal of Innovation Management, 10(1), 41-64.

De Klerk, M. n.d. Eskom: The Road to Realising our Leadership Brand – Part 1. Retrieved January 25, 2015 from www.humancapitalreview.org/content/default.asp?Article_ID=1262

De Meuse, KP, Tang, KY & Dai, G. 2009. Leadership competencies across organizational levels: a test of the pipeline model. *Journal of Management Development*, 30(4):366–380.

Dessler, G. 1976. *Organisation and Management: A Contingency Approach*. New York: Prentice-Hall.

Dessler, G. 1983. *Applied Human Relations*. New York: Prentice-Hall.

Dessler, G. 1986. *Organisational Theory, Integrating Structure and Behaviour*. New York: Prentice-Hall.

Deutsche Bank AG. 2007. *Dashboards to Measure and Manage Human Resources Risk*. Corporate Leadership Council research.

Development Dimensions International. 2008. *Leadership Development*.

Dexter, B & Christopher Prince, C. 2007. Evaluating the impact of leadership development: a case study. *Journal of European Industrial Training*, 31(8):609–625.

Du Toit, C. 2014. *The Role of Human Resources in Creating a 'Leadership Brand'*. PhD Thesis. PHD in Leadership and Change at the University of Johannesburg.

Drath, W. H., McCauley, C. D., Palus, C. J., Van Velsor, E., O'Connor, P. M. & McGuire, J. B. 2008. Direction, alignment, commitment: Toward a more integrative ontology of leadership. *The Leadership Quarterly*, 19, 635-653.

Drucker, P. 2012. Post-Capitalist Society. New York: HarperBusiness.

Dutton, J., Glynn, M. & Spreitzer, G. 2006. Positive organizational scholarship. In J. Greenhaus & G. Callanan (Eds). *Encyclopedia of career development* (pp. 641-644). Thousand Oaks, CA: Sage.

Doz, Y. & Kosonen, M. 2008. Fast Strategy. United States: FT Press.

Fernández-Aráoz, C. 2014. The Big Idea: 21st-Century Talent Spotting, Harvard Business Review, June.

Filippo, E. B. 1980. *Personnel Management* (International Student Edition). Tokyo: McGraw-Hill Kogakusha.

Fowlie, J. & Wood, M. 2009.The emotional impact of leaders' behaviours. Journal of *European Industrial Training*, 33(6), 559-572.

Friedman, T. 2005. *The World Is Flat: A Brief History of the Globalised World in the 21st Century*. London: Allen Lane.

Fulmer, R. M. & Bleak, J. L. 2008. *The Leadership Advantage: How the Best Companies are Developing Their Talent to Pave the Way for Future Success* (AMACOM ed.). New York: American Management Association.

Gandossi, R & Guarnieri, R. 2008. http://sloanreview.mit.edu/article/can-you-measure-leadership

Gardiner, J. J. 2006. Transactional, transformational, and transcendent leadership: Metaphors mapping the evolution of the theory and practice of governance. *Kravis Leadership Institute Leadership Review*, 6, 62-76.

General Motors Corporation. 2005. *Managing Investments in Rising Talent Survey*. Corporate Leadership Council research.

Geldenhuys, P. 2000. *Beyond cyberspace: Conversations in leadership* – South African perspectives. Johannesburg: Knowledge Resources.

Goldman, A. 2009. *Transforming toxic leaders*. Stanford University Press.

Goldsmith, M. 2007. *Developing your leadership brand*. Boomberg Business Week – Marshall & Friends.

Goleman, D., Boyatzis, R. & McKee, A. 2001. Primal leadership: The hidden driver of great performance. *Harvard Business Review*, no 8296, 41-51.

Groves, K. S. 2007. Integrating leadership development and succession planning best practices. Journal of Management *Development*, 26(3), 239-260.

Harter, J.K. Schmidt, F.L. & Keyes, C.L. 2002. *Well-being in the workplace and its relationship to business outcomes: A review of the Gallup Studies*. Retrieved February 20, 2014 from http://www.nhsemployers.org/ ~ /media/Employers/Documents/Retain%20and%20improve/Harter%20et%20al%202002%20WellbeingReview.pdf

Hazy, J. K., Goldstein, J. A. & Lichtenstein, B. B. 2007. Complex Systems Leadership Theory: An Introduction. In J. K. Hazy, J. A. Goldstein & B. B. Lichtenstein (Eds.). Complex Systems Leadership Theory: New Perspectives from Complexity Science on Social and Organizational effectiveness: *The Exploring Organizational Complexity Series* Vol. 1 (pp. 1-475). Mansfield: ISCE Publishing.

Hernez-broome, G. & Hughes, R. L. 2004. *Leadership development: Past, present, and future. Human Resource Planning*, 23(3), 24-32. Retrieved October 7, 2010, from http://www.ccl.org/leadership/pdf/research/cclLeadershipDevelopment.pdf.

Hersey, P. 1984. *The Situational Leader*. Johannesburg: Center for Leadership, South Africa (PE Corporate Services).

Heskett, J. L. 2008. Putting the service-profit chain to work. Retrieved August 8, 2014, from https://hbr.org/2008/07/putting-the-service-profit-chain-to-work.

Higgs, M. 2009. The good, the bad and the ugly: Leadership and narcissism. *Journal of Change Management*, 9(2):165-178.

Hogan, R. 1994. Trouble at the top: causes and consequences of managerial incompetence. *Consulting Psychology Journal*, Winter: 46(1):9-15.

Human Solutions LLC. 2005. *Measuring Your Leadership Effectiveness*. Accessed May 2012.

Human Synergystics. Undated. *Leadership /Impact*.

IBM. n.d. *Capitalizing on complexity: insights from the global chief executive officer study*. Available at http://public.dhe.ibm.com/common/ssi/ecm/en/gbe03297usen/GBE03297USEN.PDF (24 February 2014).

Idris, F. & Ali, K. A. M. 2008. The impacts of leadership style and best practices on company performances: Empirical evidence from business firms. *Total Quality Management*, 19(1-2), 163-171.

Intagliata, J, Ulrich, D & Smallwood, N. 2000. Leveraging leadership competencies to produce leadership brand: Creating distinctiveness by focusing on strategy and results. *Human Resources Planning*, 23(4):12-23.

Jackson, T. 2011. *Leader development yields ROI*. Jackson Leadership Systems Inc. Accessed May 2012.

Jaques, E. 1985. Stratification of Cognitive Complexity. Unpublished manuscript, US Army Research Institute for the Behavioural and Social Sciences.

Jaques, E. 1990. In praise of hierarchy. Harvard Business Review, 68(1), 127-134.

Jaques, E. 2005. On trust, good, and evil. International Journal of Applied Psychoanalytic Studies, 2(4), 396-403.

Jaques, E. 2006. Requisite Organization: A Total System for Effective Managerial Organization and Managerial Leadership for the 21st Century (revised 2nd ed.). Baltimore: Cason Hall.

Jaques, E. 2007. Report of a major Requisite Organisation project. In K. Shepard (Ed.). Organisation Design, Levels of Work and Human Capability: Executive Guide (pp. 163-172). Ontario, Canada: Global Organisation Design.

Jaramillo, F., Grisaffe, D. B., Chonko, L. B. & Roberts, J. A. 2009. Examining the impact of servant leadership on salesperson's turnover intention. *Leadership*, 24(3), 257-275.

Jing, F. F. & Avery, G. C. 2008. Missing links in understanding the relationship between leadership and organizational performance. *International Business & Economics Research Journal*, 7(5), 67-78.

JMW Consultants. Undated. *High Potential ROI*. Accessed May 2012.

John Maxwell company (2013). A leader's portrait. Article accessed via http://www.johnmaxwell.com.

Jones, S. 2012. *The Language of the Genes*. Fourth Estate; 2nd edition

Jung, D., Yammarino, F. J. & Lee, J. K. 2009. Moderating role of subordinates' attitudes on transformational leadership and effectiveness: A multi-cultural and multi-level perspective. *Leadership*, 20, 586-603.

Kaiser, RB & Kaplan, RE. 2006. *Outgrowing sensitivities: The deeper work of executive development*. Academy of Management Learning and Education.

Kellerman, B. 2004. *Bad Leadership: What It Is, How It Happens, Why It Matters*. Boston: Harvard Business School Press.

Kesler, G. C. 2002. Why the leadership bench never gets deeper: Ten insights about executive talent development. *HR Planning Society Journal*, 25(1), 1-28.

Kets de Vries, M. 2001. *The Leadership Mystique*. Prentice-Hall.

Kets de Vries, M. 2013. *The Eight Archetypes of Leadership*. Insead.

Kets de Vries, M, Ramo, LG & Korotov, K. 2009. *Organisational culture, leadership, change and stress*. (Faculty & research working paper). INSEAD University. Retrieved from http://www.insead.edu/facultyresearcg/reserach/doc.cfm?did=41924

Kets de Vries & Korotov, K. 2010. Developing Leaders and Leadership Development. INSEAD Faculty and Research working paper.

Kinnie, N. 1991. Human Resource Management and changes in management control systems. In J. Storey (Ed.) *New Perspectives on Human Resource Management* (p.141-153). London: International Thomson Business Press.

Leban, W. & Zulauf, C. 2004. Linking emotional intelligence abilities and transformational leadership styles. *The Leadership & Organization Development Journal*, 25(7), 554-564.

Luechauer, WBB & Locander, DDL. 2006. Building equity: Marketing executives must build leadership brand equity at a personal level. *Marketing Management*, (December):55-59.

Luthans, F. 2002. The need for and meaning of positive organizational behaviour. *Journal of Organizational Behaviour*, 706, 695-706.

Luthans, F., Avey, J. B., Avolio, B. J., Norman, S. M. & Combs, G. M. 2006. Psychological capital development: Toward a micro-intervention. *Journal of Organizational Behaviour*, 393, 387-393.

Luthans, F. & Youssef, C. M. 2007. Emerging positive organizational behavior. *Journal of Management*, 33(3), 321-349.

Marx, K & Engels, F. 1848. *Communist Manifesto*. Retrieved from https://www.marxists.org/archive/marx/works/download/pdf/Manifesto.pdf

McGregor, D. M. 1988. The Human Side of Enterprise. In H. J. Leavitt, L. R. Pondy & D. M. Boje (Eds.). *Readings in Managerial Psychology* (pp. 314-324). Chicago: University of Chicago Press.

McGuire, J. B., Rhodes, G. & Palus, C. J. 2008. Inside out transforming your leadership culture. *Leadership in Action*, 27(6), 3-7.

McGuire, J & Rhodes, G. 2009. *Transforming Your Leadership Culture*. San Francisco: Jossey-Bass.

McGurk, P. 2010. Outcomes of management and leadership development. *Journal of Management Development*, 29(5): 457–470.

McLaughlin, V. & Mott, C. 2009. Building leadership Brand Equity. Chief learning Officer, August, 46 - 48.

McLaughlin, V. & Mott, C. 2010. Leadership brand equity: HR leaders' role in driving economic value. *Strategic HR Review*, 9(4):13–19.

Melchar, D. E. & Bosco, S. M. 2010. Achieving high organization performance through servant leadership. The Journal of Business Inquiry, 2005, 74-88. Retrieved August 3, 2011, from http://www.uvu.edu/woodbury/jbi/volume9/journals/achieving_high_organization_performance_through_servant_leadership.pdf.

Mott, C & McLaughlin, V. 2009. Building leadership brand equity. *Chief Learning Officer*, 8(8):46-48.

Ng, P. K., Goh, G. G. G. & Eze, U. C. 2010. An exploratory study on leadership in a semiconductor manufacturing firm's performance. *Journal of Business and Management*, 3(2000), 231-250.

Nielson, B. 2009. *Measuring leadership effectiveness*. Accessed May 2012.

Nicoll, David, "Grace Beyond Rules: A New Paradigm for Lives on a Human Scale." In D. Adams (ed.), The Journal of Applied Business Research Volume 19, Number 3 74 Transforming Work, Alexandria, VA: Miles River Press, 1984.

Northhouse, P. G. 2004. Leadership Theory and Practice. Los Angeles: Sage Publications.

Pace, A. 2010. Unleashing positivity in the workplace. Training & Development, January, 41-44.

Padilla, A, Hogan, R & Kaiser, R. 2007. The toxic triangle: Destructive leaders, susceptible followers, and conducive environments. The Leadership Quarterly, 18:176-194.

Perth Leadership Institute. 2008. White Paper: *A Recession's role in transforming Leadership Development*. Leadership. Retrieved July 3, 2013, from http://www.perthleadership.org/Documents/WP_Recession.pdf.

Peters, T. 2009. *Re-imagine*. London: Dorling Kindersley.

Porter, M.E. 1980. *Competitive Strategy*. New York: Free Press.

Prahalad, C. K. & Krishnan, M. S. 2008. The New Age of Innovation: Driving Co-created Value through Global Networks. New Delhi: Tata McGraw-Hill.

PricewaterhouseCoopers. 2011. *Human Capital Benchmarking and Analytics*. Accessed May 2012.

Quick, JC & Nelson, DL. 2009. *Principles of organisational behaviour: realities and challenges*. 6th Ed. UK: Cengage Learning.

Reichwald, R., Siebert, J. & Moslein, K. 2005. Leadership excellence: Learning from an exploratory study on leadership systems in large multinationals. *Journal of European Industrial Training*, 29(3), 184-198.

Robbins, SP. 2014. Organisational behaviour: Concepts, controversies, and applications. 16th ed. Upper Saddle River: Prentice Hall.

F. Richard Rohs, FR. (Undated.) *Leadership development: return on investment – calculating the monetary value of the managerial assessment of proficiency program for the Georgia extension system*. University of Georgia.

Rok, B. 2009. People and skills: Ethical context of the participative leadership model: Taking people into account. *Corporate Governance*, 9(4), 461-472.

Rozwell, C. 2013. Firms battle to succeed in social. IT Online. Retrieved February 1, 2013, from http://www.it-online.co.za/2013/02/01/firms-battle-to-go-social/

Searle, T. P. & Barbuto, J. E. 2011. Servant leadership, hope, and organizational virtuousness: A framework exploring positive micro- and macro-behaviors and performance impact. *Journal of Leadership & Organizational Studies*, 18(1), 107-117.

Sharma, R. & Bhatnagar, J. 2009. Talent management – competency development: Key to global leadership. *Industrial and Commercial Training*, 41(3), 118-132.

Sinha, A & Cohen, E. 2008. Develop a winning leadership brand. *Chief Learning Officer*, 7(9):66.

Slattery, C. 2009. *Leadership darkside*. http://www.conference.co.nz/files/docs/darksideofleadership2.pdf

Slattery, C. 2009. The dark side of leadership the dark times at the top. Insight at Semann and Slattery. Discussion paper.

Sonnenfeld, J. 1983. Commentary: Academic learning, worker learning, and the Hawthorne Studies. *Harvard Business School*, 61 (3), 904-909.

Spitzmuller, M. & Ilies, R. (2010). Do they [all] see my true self ? Leaders' relational authenticity and followers' assessments of transformational leadership. *European Journal of Work and Organizational Psychology*, 19(3), 304-332.

Spreitzer, G. M. (2003). Leadership development in the virtual work place. In M. S. E. Riggio (Ed.). *The Future of Leadership Development* (pp.71-86). New Jersey: Lawrence Erlbaum Associates.

Stahl, G.K. & Bjorkman, I. 2007. Global Talent Management: How leading multinationals build and sustain their talent pipeline. *INSEAD Faculty and Research working paper*.

Stamp, G. 1985. An approach to the experience of work in "transitional" societies. *Dialogue*, 7(3), 10-23.

Stamp, G. 1989. The individual, the organisation and the path to mutual appreciation. *Personnel Management*, July, 28-31. Retrieved February 2, 2013 from http://www.bioss.name/?page_id=25

Stamp, G. 1993. *The essence of levels of work*. Bioss Southern Africa.

Stamp, G. & Isaac, J. 2009. A matrix of working relationships. In L. Ashton, P. Calitz & R. Solms (Eds.). *Wisdom@Work: An appreciation and celebration of the people, the organisations and the BIOSS ideas in Southern Africa*. Johannesburg: Knowles Publishing.

Stone, A. G. & Patterson, K. (2005). The History of Leadership Focus. Conference proceedings of the Servant Leadership Research Roundtable (pp. 1-23). Virginia Beach, VA: *School of Leadership Studies*, Regent University.

Stepshift. 2009. *Measuring the Effectiveness of Leadership Coaching*. Accessed May 2012.

Taleo Corporation. 2010. Survey Report. Corporate Learning Priorities Survey 2010.

Taylor, F. W. 1911. *The Principles of Scientific Management*. New York: Harper Brothers.

Ulrich, D & Smallwood, N. 2008. Aligning firm, leadership, and personal brand. *Leader to Leader*, Winter:24-32.

Ulrich, D & Smallwood, N. 2009. Leadership development that delivers results. *Chief Learning Officer*, March:32-35.

Ulrich, D. 2008. Develop a leadership brand. *HR Future*, August:10.

Ulrich, D. & Beatty, D. 2001. From partners to players: Extending the HR playing field. *Human Resource Management*, 40(4), 293-307.

Ulrich, D. & Johnson, J. 2011. *Demystifying the coaching mystique*. Provo, UT: The RBL Group.

Ulrich, D. & Smallwood, N. 2007a. Building a Leadership Brand. *Harvard Business Review*, July-August, 1-11.

Ulrich, D. & Smallwood, N. 2007b. *Leadership Brand: Developing Customer-Focused Leaders to Drive Performance and Build Lasting Value*. Boston, MA: Harvard Business Press.

Ulrich, D. & Smallwood, N. 2008. Aligning firm, leadership, and personal brand. *Leader to Leader*, Winter, 24-32.

Van der Merwe, L. 2006. *Leadership meta competences for the future world of work: An explorative study in the retail industry* (PHD thesis). University of Johannesburg.

Van der Merwe, L. & Verwey, A. 2007. Leadership meta-competencies for the future world of work. *South African Journal of Human Resource Management*, 5(2), 33-41.

Vardiman, P., Houghston, J. & Jinkerson, D. 2006. Environmental leadership development: Toward a contextual model of leader selection and effectiveness. *Leadership & Organization Development Journal*, 27(2), 93-105.

Veldsman, T.H. 2002. *Into the people effectiveness arena: Navigating between chaos and order*. Randburg, South Africa: Knowledge Resources.

Verwey, A., Van der Merwe, L. & Du Plessis, F. 2012. *Reshaping Leadership DNA: A Field Guide*. Randburg: Knowers Publishing.

Von Eck, C. 2007. *Change dynamics and related leadership competencies: Leading people through change and uncertainty* (PHD thesis). University of Johannesburg.

Von Eck, C. & Verwey, A. 2007. Change dynamics and related leadership competencies. *SA Journal of Human Resource Management*, 5(2), 42-50.

Vinod, S. & Sudhakar, B. 2011. Servant leadership: A unique art of leadership. Interdisciplinary *Journal of Contemporary Research in Business*, 2(11), 456-468.

Walter, F. & Bruch, H. 2008. The positive group affect spiral: A dynamic model of the emergence of positive affective similarity in work groups. *Journal of Organizational Behavior*, 29(2), 239-261.

Walumbwa, F. O., Avolio, B. J., Gardner, W. L., Wernsing, T. S. & Peterson, S. J. 2008. Authentic leadership: Development and validation of a theory-based measure. *Journal of Management*, 34(1), 89-126. Retrieved November 2, 2011, from http://digitalcommons.unl.edu/cgi/viewcontent.cgi?article=1021&context=managementfacpub&sei-

Watkinson, W. H. 1949. How welfare began: Historical survey and appreciation. In B. Thomas (Ed.). *Welfare in Industry* (pp.1-23). London: The Caxton Publishing Company.

Whittington, J. L. 2004. Corporate executives as beleaguered rulers: The leader's motive matters. *Problems and Perspectives in Management*, 3, 163-169.

Womack, J. P. 2007. Moving beyond the tool age. *IET Manufacturing Engineer*, February/March, 4-6.

Womack, J. P., Jones, D. T. & Roos, D. 1990. The Machine that Changed the World. New York: Maxwell MacMillian International.

Wren, D. A., Bedelan, A. G. & Breeze, J. D. 2002. The foundations of Henri Fayol's administrative theory. Management Decision, 40(9), 906-918.

Wilson-Starks, KY. 2003. *Toxic Leadership*. 719-534-0949, www.transleadership.com

Younger, J. & Smallwood, N. 2007. Developing your organisation's brand as a talent developer. *Human Resource Planning*, 30(2), 21-29.

Youssef, C. M. & Luthans, F. 2007. Positive organizational behaviour in the workplace: The impact of hope, optimism, and resilience. *Journal of Management*, 33(5), 774-800.

Zapf, D. 2002. Emotion work and psychological well-being: A review of the literature and some conceptual considerations. *Human Resource Management Review, 12*:237–268.

Endnotes

1 Hay/MacBer www.haygroup.com/downloads/fi/leadership_that_gets_results.pdf
2 Veldsman, 2002.
3 These could be positive or negative in terms of consequence.
4 See chapter 4 on "Leaders are people too".
5 This idea of a "critical mass" of perception is at least one of the variables in the idea that a "community" of leadership is necessary.
6 Much of this section is taken from the doctoral thesis of Charles du Toit, completed in 2014. It therefore has a slightly more "academic" slant than the rest of the chapter.
7 Marx & Engels, 1848.
8 Brooks Adams, 1913.
9 Nicoll, 1984:4.
10 Jones, 1997.
11 Drucker, 1993.
12 Dessler, 1976.
13 Dessler, 1986.
14 Bannister, 2008; Losey, 1998.
15 Dessler, 1986.
16 Taylor, 1911:11.
17 Dessler, 1983:6.
18 Watkinson, 1949.
19 Wren, Bedelan & Breeze, 2002.
20 Dessler, 1986.
21 Dessler, 1986.
22 Cubbon, 1969; Sonnenfeld, 1983.
23 Dessler 1986:41.
24 Dessler, 1986.
25 Stone & Patterson, 2005.
26 Bannister, 2008.
27 Kinnie, 1991.
28 Stone & Patterson, 2005:3.
29 Bannister, 2008.
30 Dalrymple, 2000.
31 Liker & Hoseus, 2008; Womack, 2007; Womack, Jones & Roos, 1990.
32 Whittington, 2004.
33 Friedman, 2005; Prahalad & Krishnan, 2008.
34 Bannister, 2008.
35 Ulrich & Smallwood, 2007b.
36 Peters, 2009.
37 Peters, 2009:343.
38 Fulmer & Bleak, 2008; Sharma & Bhatnagar, 2009.
39 Kesler, 2002.
40 Geldenhuys, 2004.
41 Avolio & Kahai, 2003.
42 Spreitzer, 2003:75.
43 Rozwell, 2013.
44 Bannister, 2008.
45 Chemers, 2003.
46 Dessler 1976.
47 Kellerman, 2004:5.
48 Dessler 1986:19.
49 Stoghill, 1974 in Northhouse, 2004.
50 Cubbon, 1969; Sonnenfeld, 1983.
51 Chemers, 2003; Stone & Patterson, 2005.
52 McGregor, 1988.
53 Dessler, 1986; Filippo, 1980; McGregor, 1988; Stone & Patterson, 2005.
54 Chemers, 2003; Northhouse, 2004.
55 Northhouse, 2004.
56 Hersey, 1984.
57 Kellerman, 2004:9.
58 Kellerman, 2004.
59 Kellerman, 2004.
60 Stogdill, 1963 in Northhouse, 2004.
61 Von Eck & Verwey, 2007:43.
62 Von Eck & Verwey, 2007:55.
63 Dasereau, Green & Haga, 1975
64 Northhouse, 2004:147.
65 Stone & Patterson, 2005.
66 Bhal et al, 2009.
67 Gardiner, 2006.
68 Northhouse, 2004.
69 Stone & Patterson, 2005.
70 Gardiner, 2006:71.
71 Stone & Patterson, 2005.
72 Greenleaf, 1969.
73 Whittington, 2004.
74 Liker & Hoseus, 2008:318.
75 Melchar & Bosco, 2010.
76 Von Eck & Verwey, 2007.

77 Collins, 2001.

78 Von Eck, 2007.

79 Gardiner, 2006:72.

80 Van der Merwe & Verwey, 2007.

81 Peters, 2009:429.

82 April, MacDonald & Vriesendorp, 2000:3.

83 Cameron, Quinn & De Graff, 2006:66.

84 Van der Merwe, 2006:186.

85 Cameron & Caza, 2011; Dutton, Glynn & Spreitzer, 2006.

86 Dutton et al, 2006.

87 Luthans, 2002a:59.

88 Luthans & Youssef, 2007; Luthans, Avey, Avolio, Norman & Combs, 2006.

89 Luthans & Youssef, 2007.

90 Bright, Alzola, Stansbury & Stavros, 2011.

91 Cameron, 2008a:17.

92 Cameron, 2010:51.

93 Cameron & Lavine, 2008.

94 Cameron, 2008b.

95 Pace, 2010.

96 Fowlie & Wood, 2009.

97 Jung, Yammarino & Lee, 2009.

98 Searle & Barbuto, 2011.

99 Walter & Bruch, 2008.

100 Walumbwa, Avolio, Gardner, Wernsing & Peterson, 2008

101 Luthans & Youssef, 2007

102 Avolio, Walumbwa & Weber, 2009; Bishop, 2013

103 Spitzmuller & Ilies, 2010:328.

104 Walumbwa et al, 2008:121.

105 Drath, McCauley, Palus, Van Velsor, O'Connor & McGuire, 2008.

106 Drath et al, 2008:636.

107 Avery, 2004.

108 Rok, 2009:466.

109 Jing & Avery, 2008.

110 Rok, 2009:466.

111 Lichtenstein, Uhl-bien, Marion, Seers, Orton & Schreiber, 2006:2.

112 Hazy, Goldstein & Lichtenstein, 2007.

113 Hazy et al, 2007.

114 Uhl-bien et al, 2007, in Avolio et al, 2009:431.

115 Avolio, Walumbwa & Weber, 2009.

116 Ulrich & Smallwood, 2007b.

117 Younger & Smallwood, 2007,

118 Jacobs & Lewis, 1992:17.

119 Stamp & Isaac, 2009:159.

120 Jaques, 1997.

121 Beck & Cowan, 2005.

122 Porter, 1980.

123 We often refer to judgement as "what you do when you do not know what to do, and you cannot know what to do".

124 The interplay between these three groups is an interesting way of understanding the dynamics of power and influence in social systems, and how they attempt to balance stability (continuity) and change (innovation).

125 Kets de Vries, 2013.

126 Much of this section of this chapter was sourced from Bartle (2005).See also www. cec.vcn.bc.ca

127 Re-novation means Renewal and Innovation.

128 Taleo Corporation, 2010.

129 Center for Creative Leadership, 2009a/b.

130 Corporate Leadership Council, 2009.

131 Kets de Vries et al 2009:4–9.

132 Robbins, 2014.

133 Harter, Schmidt & Keyes, 2002.

134 Goleman, 2002.

135 Cole, Boyatzis & McKee, 2004.

136 Hochschild, 1983

137 Zapf, 2002.

138 Komives, Mainella, Longerbeam, Osteen & Owenstating, 2006.

139 Adams, Henry, 1918.

140 Wilson-Starks, 2003.

141 Higgs, 2009; Hogan, 1994.

142 Slattery, 2009.

143 Padilla, Hogan & Kaiser, 2007.

144 Hogan, 1994.

145 Du Toit, 2014.

146 Collins, 2001; Idris & Ali, 2008; Melchar & Bosco, 2010; Vardiman, Houghston & Jinkerson, 2006; Vinod & Sudhakar, 2011.

147 Asree, Zain & Razalli, 2010; Buch & Rivers, 2001; McGuire, Rhodes & Palus, 2008; Yiing, Zaman & Ahmad, 2009.

148 Leban & Zulauf, 2004; Ng, Goh & Eze, 2010; Reichwald, Siebert & Moslein, 2005

149 Block, 2003; de Jong & Den Hartog,

2007; Goleman, Boyatzis & McKee, 2001; Walumbwa & Lawler, 2003.

150 Jarmillo, Grisaffe, Chonko & Roberts, 2009.

151 McLaughlin & Mott, 2010; Perth Leadership Institute, 2008.

152 Bhal, Bhaskar & Ratnam, 2009

153 Ulrich & Smallwood, 2007.

154 Amagoh, 2009; Groves, 2007a/b; Ulrich & Smallwood, 2007b; Ulrich, 2008; Verwey et al, 2012.

155 Ulrich & Smallwood, 2008.

156 Mott & McLaughlin, 2009:46.

157 Cohen & Sinha, 2008:66.

158 Ulrich & Smallwood, 2007b:201.

159 Ulrich & Smallwood, 2007a.

160 Ulrich & Beatty, 2001:294.

161 Ulrich & Johnson, 2011:2.

162 Charan et al. 2001.

163 Ulrich & Smallwood, 2008:27.

164 Ulrich & Smallwood, 2007b:8.

165 Hernez-Broome & Hughes, 2004:31.

166 Collins, 2001:41.

167 Ulrich, Younger, Brokbank & Ulrich, 2012.

168 Kets de Vries & Korotov, 2010.

169 Clutterbuck, www.davidclutterbuckpartnership.com

170 Fernández-Aráoz, 2014.

171 John Maxwell Company, 2013.

172 Stahl & Bjorkman, 2007.

173 Doz & Kosonen, 2008.

174 John Maxwell Company, 2013.

175 Language we utlise within inavit iQ.

176 Lominger International. www.kornferry.com

177 Ray, 2014. http://www.agcmass.org/news-advocacy/latest-news/engaged-employees-and-satisfied-customers-dominate-thinking-of-ceos-in-2014/

178 De Vries & Korotov, 2010.

179 Kinley & Ben-Hur, 2013.

180 Charan et al, 2001.

181 Charan & Dotter, [date]

182 Dotlich et al, 2004; Ibarra & Barbulescu, 2010.

183 Jaques 1989; Stamp 1985, 1989.

184 Watkins & Soo Hoo, 2010. http://changethis.com/manifesto/66.02.SinkOrSwim/pdf

185 Shaw & Chayes, 2011

186 De Vries & Korotov, 2010.

187 Personnel Decisions International, 2009.

188 Level requirements refer to capability, skills, time horizons and work principles/values

189 http://www.hks.harvard.edu/news-events/news/press-releases/nli-2012

190 Trademarked to inavit iQ

191 Porter, 1980.

192 IBM, 2010.

193 Mattox, J. 2012. https://www.td.org/Publications/Magazines/TD/TD-Archive/2012/02/

194 Hanley, M. n.d. www.michaelhanley.ie

195 Watkins & Soo Hoo, 2010.

196 Innovation in Leadership Development – A Mannaz White Paper www.mannaz.com

197 Corporate Leadership Council 2014.

198 De Klerk, 2014.

199 McGuire & Rhodes, 2009.

200 www.ccl.org/leadership/

201 www.mckinsey.com

202 Deloitte, 2015. www2.deloitte.com/.../Deloitte/.../ZA_global_leadership_forecast

203 Gandossi & Guarnieri, 2008.

204 Ulrich, 2008.

205 Adapted from Ulrich & Smallwood, 2008.

206 Heskett, 2008

207 Heskett, 2008.

208 Center for Creative Leadership, 2004.

209 Jacques, 1985, 1990. 2005..

210 I was very fortunate to be intimately involved in this entire process. In part, the reason for this was that I was involved in the design and implementation of the original leadership development programme that ran from 2003 to 2007.

211 All communication followed a pattern of Picture (where are we going), Purpose (why do we want to do this), Plan (how are we going to do this) and Part to Play (what is my personal role in this).

[212] As a practical consequence of this decision, we placed a consultant on site for two days per week to focus exclusively on the design and implementation of communication processes and content.

[213] In reality, and in keeping with the nature of dynamic processes, the core team had of course already started much of this design work in parallel with the strategy document being finalised. Specifically, once there was reasonable clarity on the first six sections of the strategy document we could move ahead with the design process.

[214] This simple tool is simply a list of available resources (books, articles, videos etc) linked to the leadership competencies per level. The purpose of this directory is to provide leaders with a focused, up-to-date and relevant list of resources they can access to enhance their own leadership development.

[215] We suspect that the only time it would be really possible to do things sequentially is if the client system has absolutely nothing in place.

Index

www.ingramcontent.com/pod-product-compliance
Lightning Source LLC
Chambersburg PA
CBHW080543220326

41599CB00032B/6348